THE ORIGINAL FANTASY

THE ORIGINAL FANTASY

A PRACTICAL GUIDE TO WRITING GENRE

EMILY CRAVEN

Craven Publishing

Brisbane

Contents

Dedication   ix

Original Fantasy - A Naming   x

Priori - A Beginning   xiii

Structural

Beginnings Part 1 - How to Sprinkle Your Back Story   3

Merging Characters – Cull Your Robot Clone Army   10

Character & Voice – Get it Right Before Your Character Smacks You over the Head   17

Description – Make it Dynamic   22

Setting – Filling in the Details of Your Story   28

Flashbacks - Should Your Character Remember or Relive?   37

The Importance of Beta Readers   43

Endings   58

Deepen The Story

Deepen the Story   69

The Problem of Evil   82

The Naming of Things   86

World Building – Make Believe in Five   93
Quick & Dirty Steps

Line

Beginnings Part 2 - Cast a Spell in the First   107
Line

Say it Simply - Seven Ways to Avoid   119
Overwriting

Emoting – Overwriting Round 2   133

Choosing the Right Erection – Wait! I   142
Mean 'Word'

Pacing – Avoid Interrupting a Reader's   153
Flow

Atmosphere through Description   164

Trust Your Reader's Intelligence   170

Avoiding Repetition   176

Contradictions   181

Say Something True - Clichés in Dialogue   185

Writing Dialect Subtly   192

Show Don't Tell – It's Funnier That Way   198

If You're Not a Poet, You Should Know it,   204
& Move on!

You Can Disagree... With a Valid Reason   210

Where to Now?   217
If You Enjoyed, Please, Leave a Review Online!   219
Other Books By Emily   220
Ebook Revolution The Ultimate Guide To   222
Ebook Success
About Emily   224

Dedication

Thank you Isobelle for filling my head with lessons

and always making me strive

for the simple and the true.

Original Fantasy - A Naming

At first glance the title Original Fantasy may seem a bit odd, if not a little arrogant. But I chose it for two reasons. I've been writing fantasy since I was thirteen. It was then I discovered one of my favourite authors, Isobelle Carmody, had started her book, Obernewtyn, at aged fourteen. If she could do it at fourteen then I damn well could at thirteen! My biggest fantasy at the time was that I'd get to meet Isobelle in person, that I'd be able to talk to her about how inspiring she was, how much I wanted to write like her, and ultimately, that she would be able to view my work and be proud to know she started me on my journey. This was the original fantasy sixteen years ago, and one I realised in April 2011 when Isobelle accepted me as a writing mentee for a twelve month mentorship. The manuscript we worked on was none other than that story I started when I was thirteen.

The second reason relates to what Isobelle was most anxious to impart to me during the mentorship. The ability to write a story that said something original, in a genre that had so many clichés and carbon copies. Take the competent and make it unique.

So Original Fantasy seemed apt as a title.

The mentorship was everything I'd hoped for and more, it was an honour to be accepted as a mentee for Isobelle has been known to refuse other writers in the past based on their samples. Isobelle is the author of over 30 fantasy novels for adults and children. She has such a wealth of knowledge and to have her share that understanding specifically with my manuscript, *Priori*, has been invaluable.

One thing I've learnt over the years is that a lesson never really sticks until you try to explain it to someone else. So that is the purpose of this book, to make the lesson stick, to pass the knowledge on and to give other budding genre writers, heck any writer wanting to put words to a blank page, an idea of the little details that make all the difference between a good story and a great one. It's not all fantasy based, a lot of advice applies to manuscripts in every genre. The Original Fantasy chapters were written for a blog of the same name, however, they have been reworked for this book, with extra thoughts and exercises added to help you improve and grow your own writing.

This guide is divided into three sections:

- Structural: These are considerations you need

to make on a big picture level, things that affect the readability of the novel as a whole.

- Deepen The Story: These lessons look at deepening your story beyond the clichés and tropes that are found in so many genre novels.

- Line: These are edits that need to be made on a small scale level. This is all about elevating your novel from good to great. These lessons aim to tighten prose, paint a crystal clear picture and make the sentences so smooth a reader can't stop reading.

Fortunately for you (though possibly reputation damaging for me!) you get to see live examples of all the various oversights I made in my own manuscript and the reasons why they needed to change. Though, for the sake of my pride, at the end of each chapter I'm also going to present my 'Golden Moments', passages Isobelle deemed beautifully and concisely written. It will make me feel better about my many writing boo-boos...

Hopefully my past mistakes will help you be a better writer.

Priori - A Beginning

Throughout this guide you are going to see a lot of references to my fantasy manuscript, *Priori*, which I worked on with Isobelle during our mentorship. Out of context, these piece of text might seem... perplexing. So I thought I'd give you a short introduction to the text and how it's evolved over the years before we dive into those juicy, juicy lessons.

The Story

Hunted by the Kraken, the sinister leader of the Ruhle Empire, Beverly Jordan must control her powers, known only as the Priori, to survive. Believing her powers fit only for destruction and ruin, Beverly and her brother Charlie set off on a journey to find the fabled haven of Creana. An underwater world where one can learn to split the fabric of time and manipulate the Lines of Power, where winged Alaequines soar through the air and the Shadows lurk in waiting for someone to release them.

Will Beverly escape the grasping clutches of the Kraken? Or is she destined to become his weapon?

Priori was the very same novel I started when I was thirteen and has an eclectic feel to it that seemed to be influenced by whatever author I was loving at the time, whether that be Isobelle, J.K. Rowling, Garth Nix, Dianna Wynne Jones or Tamora Pierce (all still favourites!). The novel has been rewritten dozens of times over the years and deals with the idea of not letting the past define you, and turning the things that have come to you along dark paths into forces for good in the future.

In this world magick is accessed via the manipulation of an invisible grid of natural magic called the Lines of Power. Most magick users only have a sliver of inner magick. Well, all except our main character Beverly, who accidentally became the host of the Priori powers after the Kraken ripped them from the bodies of thousands of magick users. Beverly's extra abilities make her very powerful, and also dangerous.

The Evolution

The first draft (or ten) were frankly awful, but as my skills have improved, so too has the novel improved to the point I felt ok using it as my main project in my mentorship with Isobelle in 2012. In an effort to build up my profile and potential audience, I then blogged the lessons in a shortened form on my Original Fantasy site (now Craven Stories). Keen to keep that momentum going I wheedled my way into the hearts of several very talented actor friends to create a serialised audio podcast version of the novel. And from that project, this guide was born like a new star, in a burst of combustible gas and frenzied activity.

Structural

BEGINNINGS PART 1 - HOW TO SPRINKLE YOUR BACK STORY

We've all read a book that starts with a prelude, a prologue, or an author's note basically saying, "Right, this shit went down a while ago, it's important, remember it, now here's the story built on this information dump." It's difficult in speculative fiction (or in any novel really) to figure out how to feed the necessary information to the readers. A potted history at the start, complete with red flags identifying the bad guy, the unfortunate victims and possible heroes/heroines, seems the simplest way to get rid of all the Telling and be free to describe you main story.

Take for example Isobelle Carmody's, *Obernewtyn*. Though it was shortlisted for Book of the Year, her prologue was one of the things picked on by the critics. It was noted to be an efficient, yet rather soulless way to give information. All that information and then a new history on top are difficult to take in so early in a book. Particularly if you are writing for a Young Adult (YA) audience. Open your closest YA book and see how few, if any, have an information dump at the start of the book. It's because filtering in the back story throughout the novel is more dynamic, and much more surprising when the reader finally gets that piece of information they've been waiting for.

Anticipation and intrigue is what keeps a reader turning the page. Why would you give that up? I can hear you saying, "Well clearly because we can't be bothered!" But if you want to excel as a writer – and actually gain the attention of a publisher – then you'd better start learning to be subtle, and weave in that back story. Another thing to keep in mind is this means the reader learns information as the character learns information, helping them identify more fully with your cast of heroes. Again, going back to it being more dynamic, we can see the character's reaction to finding out the information and use the back story not only to inform but to build on characterisation.

In *Priori*, I originally had a prelude and was told to get rid of it by the first editor I ever hired. "There's no action! You have to start in a moment of intrigue or suspense. You're not going to keep people's attention if they think you're going to just stuff information into their head." So

I switched to feeding my readers the back story by having Charlie, the brother of my heroine, Beverly, telling the story. Below is Isobelle's comment on that change:

"You are using the brother as a conduit – this is clever because it means that the story can be told as they are doing things together. The trouble is it is coming out like a little lecture. What I would ask you to consider is if it is necessary right now. Because if the story can work without it, then you put off offering the information, because you may well find that it is told better by implication and clues which the reader themselves must build up into a story. My advice here might be to remove the entire back story (i.e. father's story/back story for the Priori etc.) and focus on the abortive attempt to escape, the testing, what these events reveal about the mother, the brother and the main character, and making the world feel very real. The readers will simply come to this point afire with the desire to know exactly what the Priori is and how it got into the main character, and who sets up the testing and why the mother is so cold etc."

~ Isobelle Carmody

I had merely changed from an information dump by a narrator at the start, to the brother dumping the information on young Beverly and the reader. The back story needed to be integrated even further into the tale, dripping bits of information about the world, the heroine's father and the past in an intriguing rather than text book way. In essence the beginning of your fantasy, or any novel, *should focus on characterisation rather than history*. Your task in the early chapters is to make your character riveting, so readers *care* what happens to them.

For example, I originally had Charlie tell Beverly the name of the place they were escaping to in his info dump lecture. In my rewrite I took that information and put it five chapters further into the tale:

She hesitated, "We... are from Creana."

Straining to look over Charlie's shoulder, I stared at her. The name meant nothing.

"Creana?" Charlie drew in a sharp breath. It was as though the weight of the world had been lifted off his shoulders. He finally let me wiggle past him to stand at his side.

Tightening the hold on my sword hilt, I flicked my eyes between the strangers and Charlie. "Someone needs to explain. What's Creana?" My voice sounded harsh.

"It's where we are going," Charlie replied, eyeing the two strangers before us.

"But you said we were going to find your man, El..."

"Elliott," supplied Charlie. "Yes. He guards the map that will lead us there."

"Then where is it?"

Charlie raised his eyebrows at the pair, arms crossed.

"Under water," said the girl, large eyes earnest. "Creana is a city. The salt water acts like an armour against the Kraken's weapon."

Not a sound passed between us as we stood off, one pair against

the other. Charlie's hands fell to his sides, away from the hidden
blades in his sleeves. "Well done, you passed," said Charlie.

~ Priori – Rewrite

As you can see I used the information to create tension
in the scene and bring out the characters more fully. It was
such a simple bit of information. I could have dumped it
in a prologue, but then I would never have ended up with
this deliciously tense scene.

Exercise

Do you have a prologue describing the back story to your
novel? Or a particularly large lecture from one character to
another known as an info dump (if you're spending more
than two pages explaining some sort of history from one
character to the next, that qualifies)? Let's see if we can work
this information into the narrative a bit better.

- Step 1: Pull out the various pieces of history
  from this scene/prologue and then ask yourself
  if they are *key* to a particular plot twist, break
  through, or future solution. Does your narrative
  still make sense with these pieces of narrative
  missing? If the information isn't needed for a
  plot twist or break through, can you throw that

information away (avoiding an info dump all together)? Or maybe you can throw the whole scene away. If the information is needed, is it needed right this minute?

- Step 2: If this scene contains other important elements, like building characterisation, or establishing societal norms (e.g. Steampunk decoration, patriarchal society etc.), and as such you *can't* get rid of the scene entirely, make sure you leave only *one or two* pieces of key back story/historical info in that scene.

- Step 3: Then, setting the other pieces of background info to one side, go through the rest of your novel and find the point at which a character *must* know a particular piece of information.

- Step 4: Then look for a scene as close to this point as possible where you can insert the information and inform the character.

- Step 5: Now try to incorporate the information as naturally as possible into that scene (this may need a rewrite or invention of a new scene). Use this as an opportunity to: create a scene with great conflict, to increase the tension, or show character growth (or change a character's motivations).

The below Golden Moment could have been one such throwaway line: you see something out of the corner of your eye, you think you imagined it. But what if it was the fourth or fifth time you had seen something? Did it mean you were more traumatised than you realised? This little golden moment builds tension from that and raises questions about the main character's objectivity, and sanity, while also setting up a later scene.

Golden Moments

"Yes, a pumpkin. They have such simple lives. They don't have to deal with-" A prickling sensation on the back of my neck stopped me in my tracks as a shadow shifted in the steady globe light to my left. Again. All week I had been unable to shake the feeling that I was being watched. Each tell-tale prickle had me jerking my head to look behind, or around a corner only to see shadows shift in the balanced light. In some cases I could make out a vaguely human shaped darkness just sidle away. I had a sneaking suspicion that all my subterfuge on the surface had resulted in my mind developing more than one batty illusion to fuel my paranoia addiction.

~ Priori

MERGING CHARACTERS – CULL YOUR ROBOT CLONE ARMY

My first drafts tend to be like a Sparta movie, a cast of thousands that during the course of the writing process must eventually die at the pointy end of a sword. Like terracotta warriors, many of my initial characters performed exactly the same function, they were just painted a slightly different colour blue. Clone characters rampaged through the draft of *Priori* in an attempt to 'prove' the main character's popularity/unpopularity, but all they left behind was weak characterisation strewn like dismembered body parts (hail Sparta!).

By consolidating 'clone' characters, characters who basically perform the same function, you can build yourself a super-character whose superpower is to thicken your thinly stretched cast and ultimately, make your reader like them more than your protagonist.

I first realised I was cloning characters when Isobelle picked on a particularly vague piece of *Priori* draft:

Separated neatly from Fidleton by the flowing mass, I was herded along to the main chute with a crowd of students who lived in the castle. In the end I followed a pretty fourth year apprentice, called Kara Datal to the gathering room. Kara lived in the city out to sea called Gnarann, but her parents chose to send her to board at Oceana instead of attending Gnarann's own Academy. Kara's fine bone structure and beautiful short, blond hair highlighted her brown eyes and went hand in hand with her very compelling voice.

~ Priori – Draft

"Seems to me we are introduced to this girl too briefly and incidentally- either she is important for us to know more, in which case have them talk properly and interact on the way through the crowd, or don't get into her. It doesn't need to be long, but to get so much information it would need to be decisive and you might need to put them in a line somewhere, and have the other girl recognise from the coat that they are the same year or something."

~ Isobelle Carmody

I had treated Kara as a stand in, a piece of set design

until I was ready to fill her out with my 3D fiction printer (could you imagine if that were real? The types of killer unicorns you could make with that thing...). Similarly, I had another character whose job it was to be my main character, Beverly's, roommate. Other than being super smart (and if I'm honest, a Hermione doppelganger) she contributed a whole jar full of nothing to the story. She was there to give the Academy a boarding school/college feel. It felt like I was killing my children when I made the decision to merge Kara and this roommate into a single character a reader would actually give a toss about. I needed characters I'd get hate mail about if I killed them with my pointy storytelling sword. When I did that I was able to give a proper introduction to this important character who became a mentor to Beverly:

Separated neatly from the Adept by the flowing mass, I was herded along to the main chute with a crowd of students who lived in the castle. With trepidation I eyed the medallions around me looking for another which had the glittering red ruby as its largest stone. "Where's a Firefre when you need one?" I muttered.

"Generally above you," replied a wry voice. "But in this case, behind."

I strained to look over my shoulder, the press of bodies too thick to turn. In the corner of my eye I saw a wave of short blond hair and one large brown eye. Then the crowd shifted and I couldn't see her. "How do I get to the Firefre—" I began then stumbled forward as the person before me disappeared in a rush of air.

I collided with a pale faced student on my right as they said, "Level three."

My body shot upward with the student, our surrounds spun alarmingly, and hair was thrust across my face by the whirlwind of the chute. The third floor corridor lurched into focus and I stood once again on a solid floor. A pair of small hands gripped my arms and led me off the platform as my stomach rebelled.

"At least you came to the right floor," said the same compelling voice from the crowd. The hands released me and a pretty young woman stepped in front of me, dainty hand palm up in greeting. "I'm Kara Datal."

Reaching out a shaking hand I touched my palm to hers then wiped the sweat from my forehead with a sleeve. "I'm Beverly Jordan and I'm most definitely lost."

Kara's brown eyes crinkled in a smile, her fine bone structure framing a radiant grin. "Well that's convenient; I thought I'd have to wait until you got back to the room to introduce myself."

I stared at her for a moment then the flame of memory ignited. "You're my roommate!"

She bowed. "In the flesh. Good thing I'm able to guide you, or else who knows when we would have met. It's harder to find a closet you accidentally lock yourself in than leading you to the gathering place."

I flushed, reflecting that I was more likely to end up on the roof than a closet if left to find the gathering place myself.

~ Priori – Draft

I also had two people who had taken a fairly irrational dislike to Beverly, a boy and a girl, unrelated but both doing the same thing – making life difficult for her. There was no need to expend effort making them *both* interesting if I could combine them into one and make a super-character.

Remember, more is not always better, and unless you're original in your characterisation a cast of thousands is only going to make you look like a Hollywood flop. Watch out for those sneaky clones, if there's one thing I've learnt it's that their genetic make-up is weak and unstable, don't let them form a robot army and kill your novel in its sleep.

Exercise

Identifying clone characters takes practise. Sometimes, as with a lot of aspects of life, you can identify them in other people's work better than your own. For example, Lord of the Rings has lots of 'wise old men' and comic relief 'sidekicks' that may have created a greater connection with readers if they were a single character. So use the below exercise for practice.

- Step 1: Pick up your favourite story and see if you can identify any clone characters that could have been merged to create a stronger character. This will help you get into the analytical mode for step two, identifying the clone characters in your own work.

- Step 2: Make a list of the characters in your own work, both major and minor. What are their motivations, fears, and their 'role' in the story? And by role I don't mean 'the fisherman's wife', that's a relationship designation. I mean, what is her role in the story? Is she the keeper of the fisherman's secrets, or the person who goads the fisherman's nasty or nice side?

- Step 3: Take any characters that look like they're performing similar roles, and see if there's a way you can merge them into a single, more complex character. Your chick-lit heroine doesn't need 4 friends to shop and gossip with, she probably is only tight with one or two and they are the ones that push her decision making/ motivation buttons.

I had fallen into the clone trap in previous versions of *Priori* particularly at the start of the novel where I was trying to establish how my character was different through her ability to speak to animals. But it was a cast of half a dozen animals who just quipped passing jokes and didn't add much else. So during my rewrite for the mentorship, and the below Golden Moment, I decided instead to showcase Beverly's relationship with only one of the animals, her horse. Sarsha became one of Beverly's only 'friends' on the surface and the focal point for amusing observations on human behaviour.

Golden Moments

"What is the two-legger doing?" Sarsha's mind voice asked curiously, with a sharp flick of her tail.

"Trying to communicate," I thought back.

"It is doing a bad job," she observed, before returning her attention to her bag of oats.

~ Priori

CHARACTER & VOICE – GET IT RIGHT BEFORE YOUR CHARACTER SMACKS YOU OVER THE HEAD

You'd think finding the right voice for your character wouldn't be hard. I mean you can speak, you can sing off-key, you know that your friends speak differently, you've got that memory of the conversation you all had last week about apostrophes that gives you a wealth of expressions and tones to work with. Too bad you only remember the gist of what they were saying; it just doesn't come off right when you word it. It doesn't sound like them. Perhaps you're better off acting; at least you can hear that Scottish twang you're trying to infuse in your words.

Everyone phrases things differently, chooses the same words and rearranges them in a way that is their own, so when you hear the words spoken you can pick exactly who it is. Blindfolded and upside down. Yes, real world dialogue is *that* different.

Many times you'll find the right character voice doesn't kick in until part way through writing your novel, when you're in the thick of the story. Then your character throws a tantrum and asks why you've been paraphrasing this whole time rather than damn well writing down what they say! One of the problems with fantasy in particular is writers choose an archaic, poetic way of having characters express themselves and it's so stiff it crushes all the vivacity out of them, like you've kicked them out of an aeroplane and used what's left. A flat pancake of a character.

It is with absolute authority that I can say having two eighteen year olds and a twenty-three year old on top of you is about as comfortable as metal underwear.

~ Beverly Jordan, Priori

The example above was a favourite of Isobelle's, she correctly identified it as the point when my character finally got some kick and the character stopped being a carbon copy of every other fantasy heroine. The sentence was very real, and the emotion felt right. The problem was the sentence sat strangely alongside the more stilted and formal things Beverly did and said. Even after the point the *real* Beverly appeared, I had written a sort of formalness into her interactions like the example below:

"Someone didn't learn any manners as a child." I glared at the girl's receding back.

~ Priori – Draft

This sounds WAY too old for a teenage character, and much too formal. If I were to match this to the spirited character on the previous page, Beverly should be saying something along the lines of, "Clumsy cow!" or, "Who was that?!"

The voice in the first example was feistier and more interesting than the girl who I had made meek and scared and occasionally pitiful. The question was why? Why did I make her that way to start with? I dug deep (and had to use an Olympic stadium floodlight to see) but realised I'd thought it made for better emotional drama. What I didn't realise, even though each of my favourite authors does this, was that having a feisty character scared, when they are not usually so, or having a brave character devastated, is very strong. Even if I wanted the book to encompass her journey from weakness to strength I still needed moments when I allowed her future strength to be foreshadowed.

So when I did my last rewrite, I focused on Beverly's

voice, her real one, and made sure it was present. I then did the same for all of the characters in the *Priori*. The Golden Moment for this chapter perfectly captures the voices and relationship between the twins, and Beverly's friends, Cypress and Satinay.

Exercises

To get the true voice of your character you don't have to make lists of words/phrases they use, or make up playlists of YouTube videos in hours of research (though you can if you're so inclined). All you need to do is a little bit of sifting through the story you currently have using the simple exercise below.

- Step 1: Go to your latest work in progress (WIP) and find the first bit of main character dialogue that truly shows the *real* character, the one sentence where you read it and get a sense that "Yes! This is them!" Copy and paste it into a word document.

- Step 2: Find at least 2-3 *more* sentences that really shout at you as being full of character and put them in this document.

- Step 3: Print it out, stick it to your wall! Now, go back through your piece, comparing the tone of each to those sentences to the rest of the

---

dialogue for that character and adjust accordingly so that the character rings true throughout the whole piece.

To give you an illustration, below is one of my favourite examples of a character jumping out of the page. It really sets the tone for the stern, and rather pedantic father:

"But names are important!" the nursemaid protested.

"Yes," said Quillam Mye. "So is accuracy."

~ Fly by Night, Frances Hardinge

Golden Moments

"Idiot! When will you stop believing everything I say! I know she's here because the metal is glowing. She must have an ancient relic, one of the ones made when we still lived on the surface."

"We shouldn't be here in the first place; we wouldn't be here at all if you hadn't been spying... and it could just as well be a he. I've heard him referred to as a male."

"Most males are referred to as 'he'," came the girl's quick response.

~ Priori

DESCRIPTION – MAKE IT DYNAMIC

Before the mentorship I had a habit of separating description from action. "I had a habit." It sounds like an addiction. I suppose it was in the way that addicts are in denial about it happening. But once Isobelle staged my 'intervention' I was spotting it all over the place.

For some reason I'd gotten it into my head that I needed to build a picture before the character did anything. But without anything actually happening, your story kind of grinds to a standstill and your perfect, original description starts to fall on bored ears. At best, the reader will skip the description to get to the action, never really knowing what the character, or scenery looks like, and hence not building a strong connection with them or the book. At worst, they'll stop reading.

Thriller author J.C. Hutchens says, if you can have the same scene or conversation walking down the hall as you can standing still, then go for the walk down the hall every time. Because if your characters are in motion, the story is in motion.

The same can be said for description. If you can weave the description into the action, then the pace does not suddenly hit a brick wall and fall on its bum. Below I separated my description of these magickal (yes with a 'k') creatures from the action, and recited their history rather than have my main character Beverly interact with the woman next to her. In the recast I tried to follow Isobelle's suggestion of describing the creatures as they served, and making Beverly have a real conversation so the reader could meet the friendly person next to her more fully. Which do you think is more dynamic?

The servitors were most obviously magickal creatures. Small multilayered, pointed ears complimented three thin red strips down their elongated nose. A thick white mane and tufted tail merged into the soft tan fur. They were called Frijipuffs. Cheerfully they brought out the food, singing softly as they did so. Adept Fidleton informed me that they usually lived in caves on the side of mountains, hence why they appeared so timid. However the unavoidable events caused by the Ruhle occupation had sent all magickal creatures into hiding. The Frijipuffs had no place they could retreat to so some used Oceana as their permanent residence in exchange for services.

EMILY CRAVEN

~ Priori – Draft

The servitors when they appeared were most obviously magickal creatures. They brought out the food, singing softly and balanced a plate on each furry hand. One of the little creatures came up next to me and reached over to place the serving plates in the middle of the table. Its small multilayered, pointed ears were complimented by three red strips down its elongated nose. A thick white mane and tufted tail – draped delicately over one arm – merged into the soft tan fur.

"These lovely servitors are known as Frijipuffs." Adept Fidleton reached out to place some sliced Vregietop and steaming pie on the plate in front of her. "I'm sure you wouldn't have come across them before."

I shook my head. "No, I've never even heard of them in any books I've read."

She dug into her food with relish. "No you wouldn't, they were very timid when they were on the surface. They use to live in caves on the side of a sheer mountain. But the Ruhle occupation sent every magickal creature into hiding."

"Why are they serving the meals then?" I asked, watching three of the Frijipuffs perform a little harmony, their expression joyous, before filing back through the small door.

"They had nowhere to retreat that would protect them from the Ruhle's weapon, so some use Oceana as their permanent residence in exchange for services. Just like students are expected to help maintain Creana to pay for part of their studies."

~ Priori – Rewrite

24

Now the reader knows a little more about Adept Fidleton who has never been properly introduced and would have been a 'talking hand' otherwise. It may be easier for you to recount the information, but it's more boring for the reader. It's like food, you don't want them to rearrange the meal you spent six hours (or six years!) cooking, you want them to hoe in!

The 'Golden Moment' at the end of this chapter was marked as such by Isobelle because it integrated description with action. A fiddly, time consuming task, but worthwhile to see your readers power through those pages.

Exercise

Do you describe a character before the action? Chances are it's slowing the pace of your novel considerably as you meticulously sketch every feature of your character. Remember, a character is more than their visual description! A well-chosen piece of dialogue may result in a much stronger impression than a whole paragraph of description. Similarly, a landscape description will become more vivid, and seem to hold more movement if you are interspersing it between interactions.

The below exercise will give you some skill in rearranging your words to create this more dynamic storytelling.

- Step 1: Find a scene in your book where there are long slabs of description without action or dialogue (or if you want to work specifically on characterisation, a section where you fully describe a character before diving into the interaction).

- Step 2: Now, rewrite this section so that the description is interspersed with action and dialogue. In this way you are increasing the pace of your story, giving you a greater hold on the reader's interest. After all, it's the characters we care about, not the configuration of the living room, or the precise placement of buttons on a coat.

Golden Moments

"Nuts, dead end again." Satinay's finger jabbed out to poke the very solid brick wall.

"What does the map say?" I shifted my heavy satchel from one shoulder to the other for the umpteenth time.

"Completely blank." Cypress held the carefully folded piece of paper flat. His medallion lay on the bare skin of his chest, just visible above the v of his shirt. Finger crooked, he hooked a Line of Power embedded in the paper and scrolled through the various sections of the castle map.

"So we've wandered into a forbidden section again?" I let my bag fall to the ground with a thud, slumping against the offending dead end.

A nose appeared suddenly on the wall next to me followed by a shaggy beard and then the slouched body of a third year apprentice emerged, walking through the wall as though it were made of cobwebs. He scowled at us, eyebrows bunched in suspicion before shuffling down the corridor.

~ Priori

SETTING – FILLING IN THE DETAILS OF YOUR STORY

When you're first creating a story, getting the bare bones of it down, you're going to be a little light on the detail. Why? Because holding both the plotline and the world building in your head at once will make it explode. It's a scientifically proven fact. No writer ever expects to turn out a first draft that is instantly publishable because we know it's hard to fully realise the shape of things until it's written down. So it's fine to skimp on the details in the first draft. It's even fine on the fourth, fifth and sixth drafts. But at some point you've got to fill in those sections that skim over the meat of a story. You may not have had the time while beating that 'dreaded blank page' to fully sketch out the dragon with the golden beard and the three nipples. But once it's on the page, you've got to go back and colour in that sketch.

However, don't overdo the description! As always keep things simple, a few choice words paint a clearer picture then an entire page. In a similar vein to the previous chapter, extra descriptive words slow down the pace of a story just as surely as an entire descriptive passage. As you may know when you hear older, wrinklier family members talking about doing activities you'd rather not know about, there is such a thing as too much information. Colour it in but don't soak the paper in ink until it's a pulpy mess.

The most important thing to keep in mind when filling these 'place holder' phrases is to know *where you are*. It sounds fairly simple, you've got eyes in real life (if not, how are you reading this?), you've seen mountains, lakes, forests, houses, sagging bottoms and false teeth, you know what they all look like. But can you explain that scene to someone who is blind folded, has head plugs in, and a blocked nose? You get the picture...

Apart from the fact that imagining a scene and standing in one are vastly different things, the main problem is you don't consciously think about your perspective when you're observing things in the real world. The brain fills in details you can't see from your physical position with memories of previous exploration. Your brain knows right from left but won't point it out to you as you study your surroundings. Heck, your brain's not a tour guide – "On *your left you'll see a rubbish bin, and if you look to your right, a tree*". It just sees "*green bin, lid open. Tree with stringy bark, thin leaves, no shade, potential Drop Bear site*". These subconscious thoughts of placement and orientation ground us, and in fiction they need to be explicitly pointed out because the reader doesn't have their back brain to fill in the orientation side of things.

So keeping this in mind, I split the lesson of "Knowing Where You Are" into three categories:

1: Explicit Description

As I said above, over describing leads to TMI and readers taking an afternoon nana-nap over your book. You need to be both consistent in your description from paragraph to paragraph (beware the Microsoft Word synonym function here) and explicit in what the terrain actually looks like. *"He saw her and ran down the green slope into her heaving bosom,"* isn't going to cut the reader-visualisation mustard. Below is an example from my original *Priori* draft. I didn't really have a clear picture of the area Beverly was in and had described it differently in two separate scenes, making my lack of clarity very obvious to the reader.

Bursting through an embankment of trees I descended the gentle slope on the other side.

~ Priori – Draft

ORIGINAL FANTASY

"Before you called it a bank of trees. Be careful to be explicit and to really visualise your terrain to avoid repetition."

~ Isobelle Carmody

You should add this to your writing rules – Repetition is the Devil. Make T-shirts, shoes and other merchandise sporting this slogan until this is burnt into your brain. Hopefully that way your scenes will also be burnt into your brain and you can create them with all the clarity of a photograph without repeating yourself. Below is yet another example of not fully realising the landscape before I described it:

We entered the iron gates of Oceana Academy and came to the wooden door of the school. Intricate silver patterns swirled across the wood. Two flaming torches were placed in brackets on either side of the door, their reflected glow making the silver undulate like liquid. Madam Carter rang the silver bell hanging next to the door. A stone sphinx stood on either side of the broad main steps. Each was about two metres high.

~ Priori – Draft

"Where are these steps in relation to the door? If the door is at the top, you need to say so and maybe the scene with the sphinxes

should happen before they mount the steps and you describe the ringing of the bell."

~ Isobelle Carmody

2: Character View Point

There are times when you'll want to fully describe the complex landscape you have created, lovingly dropping in every detail. FYI, I'll let you in on a little tip. I don't need to know every piece of laundry hanging on your talking hamster's washing line. I get it, your character wears and washes clothes, that's great, but do I need that to visualise a scene in which the clothes-wearing hamster is mauled by a fox in the light of a blood moon? Besides which, whether you like it or not, your character is not omnipresent (unless you've written the story with an omnipresent narrator and only a handful of elite authors can pull that baby off). Logic dictates the character cannot 'see' all of your elaborate set design, because they bodily only inhabit a single space and perspective.

In the middle of the city was a large, deep blue lake which overflowed at the far end to some unseen terrace below.

~ **Priori – Draft**

"If it is unseen she cannot know it will overflow to a terrace. Better to just say it overflows or spills from sight."

~ Isobelle Carmody

*

It was the largest room I had ever laid eyes upon, so massive that only half the hall seemed to be used regularly.

~ Priori – Draft

"She can't know this."

~ Isobelle Carmody

*

This morning everyone was sitting at one of the larger tables.

~ Priori – Draft

"Again, she cannot know that 'this morning' might not be as other mornings since she has never been here before, nor would she be likely to say 'everyone' because it sounds too familiar. She would say something like, "There were a group of people sitting at

one of the larger tables, and as we drew near, I saw that one of them was Master Elitree. He rose and...").”

~ Isobelle Carmody

You need to keep in mind, *who* is standing *where* in the scene and *what* part of that scene the character can observe from this position.

3: Once You're in, You're in

Know that while you *can* address the reader, it sometimes isn't wise to. Characters inhabit a tale, and a particular world. If they start addressing the reader directly, then they are encroaching upon the real world, a sure fire way to drop kick your reader out of the narrative. The purpose of a story is to entertain and draw readers into a whole new plane of existence, not draw attention to the fact that the characters are imaginary and that Mad Hatter Tea Party is just words on a page.

Riding without stopping all day, nothing to eat the food having run out the day before... well, one could imagine my mood at this moment.

~ Priori – Draft

"This air of the main character addressing the reader in an intimate aside is a little jarring- either do it all along or don't do it, there is no in between."

~ Isobelle Carmody

Applying these three points will allow you to expand your skeleton story such that the character stays within the limits of their location. If you know the exact limits of what your character can and cannot see, you may have a draft that can survive a publisher's slush pile.

Exercises

To get a feel for how to position your character well in a scene (and hence your reader), try this exercise:

- **Step 1:** Pick a scene/chapter. On a piece of paper note who the main POV character is in this section. Block out where they are positioned (standing, sitting, walking) throughout the whole scene.

- **Step 2:** Now look at any description of landscape or space, and compare it to where they are positioned at that time. Could they note all of what you have described from where they are?

- Step 3: Then check the description to see if you have been specific enough. Where exactly is that desk placed? What direction does that flying ship travel in relation to the character? They are unlikely to know if things are east, west, north or south for example, but they can quickly identify it is moving to the right or left.

- Step 4: If there are inconsistencies in how your character sees their world, rewrite your scene/chapter to fix this.

In the below Golden Moment the location descriptions are very simple, but clear and concise, sketching the room without removing the reader's pleasure of adding their own detail.

Golden Moments

One, a heavily built man, with a large, neatly trimmed moustache and heavy lidded eyes, stood at attention in the middle of the room. Through the window I could see four more brown clad soldiers in the front courtyard, bored and bothered.

~ Priori

FLASHBACKS - SHOULD YOUR CHARACTER REMEMBER OR RELIVE?

How vivid is your imagination? When you think back to that time when you told your sister it was tradition to face-plant into the birthday cake, are you remembering the event, repeating the words of a pre-prepared story, or are you reliving the screams and the neon blue bubblegum rivers tracking down her happy face? Just as past events make you who you are, scenes of past events are key to a reader finding out about a character's motivations and what makes them do the embarrassing things they do. As writers, we are the masters of time travel, if we want to hold back that life-scarring experience our character had involving a chipmunk, some coconut oil and very loose pant-legs until half way through a novel, we can.

When we revisit our own past we do it in one of two ways, telling ourselves or others a sequence of events via retrospective remembrance, or by reliving every vivid detail in our heads, leaving us standing in the real world like an addled grandparent with a faraway look and a silly smile on our face. Remembering is looking back on a moment with very clear intruding thoughts from a smug, present self, imbued with hindsight. Reliving is being in *the moment*; fully experiencing every piece of that scene without any interruption from the know-it-all you are now. Basically reliving is a 'flashback' in novel terms, remembering is you telling someone else (or reminding yourself) about it. When you are creating a story, it is one of the hardest things to decide whether you should have your character remember or relive a particular scene.

One of my clearest memories is her reflection staring at the object in her hand.

~ Priori – Draft

"You need to decide if she is remembering or reliving. I have this problem a lot – I'd suggest she relive it first and then have her think about it afterwards while riding with her brother under the brilliant sky. Right now what we most want to know most is what the Priori is/are."

~ Isobelle Carmody

So how do you choose which angle to take with those embarrassing/scarring/overly-familiar-furry-friend flashbacks? After considering Isobelle's response above I've come to the conclusion that remembering is a passive version of storytelling, whereas reliving brings the reader into the past with the character, feeling emotions and events in such vivid detail that they, like the character, can look back on it like a memory of their own life. This isn't to say remembering can't be used to great effect.

A question to ask yourself if you're undecided is this: if your character is recounting their chipmunk experience to someone else, do you want the second character's reaction to be a large part of the story? Then remembering will work better in that instance because the purpose of the scene is the bonding/interaction between the two characters, not deepening the reader's connection to the protagonist. However, with remembering you should be cautious, as you don't want to over emote with your secondary character.

For me, flashbacks now will always be about reliving 'the chaos of the birthday party' as I want to bond my readers as strongly as possible to my characters.

Exercises

As with many exercises, sometimes it's better to practise on someone else's story than your own. In this exercise I urge you to take a look at one of your favourite novels by another author, and remake it.

- Step 1: Pick up your favourite novel and find a scene where the main point of view character is remembering something or reliving/ experiencing a flashback out of the normal chronological order.

- Step 2: Now rewrite that scene in the opposite way (e.g. If it's a relived scene rewrite it as a remembering scene).

- Step 3: Step back and compare the original to your rewrite (in a literary pros and cons list). What sort of information comes out in the rewrite? How has it affected the pace? Is it more engaging for the reader or does it distance things? In your opinion, was the original scene written the best way at that point in the story?

In the next Golden Moment, I introduce the two chatty stone sphinxes that guard the entrance to the Academy that Beverly attends. I used this scene as a way to inform Beverly that the date of a dragonet hunt she had been training for was finally set. It would have been a fairly boring scene having an official such as the captain give the information straight to Beverly. But by having the sphinxes 'remember' the information they overheard, we are drawing out the tension of Beverly's reaction and exploring the relationship of the sphinxes between each other and to Beverly, presenting the information in a much more entertaining way.

Golden Moments

"Well if you'll excuse us, we're off to lunch," said Satinay, edging forward.

"Ah food," Tutankamon stretched luxuriously, one massive stone fore-claw effectively blocking our escape. "Never tried it before, have we Cleo?"

"Wouldn't really know what was good, Mon," Cleo agreed, "Can't eat the students."

We froze as both sphinxes regarded us for several moments, their heads cocked, pointed marble teeth edging past grey lips.

"No, I suppose not. Elitree would not be pleased. Besides, then we'd lose the view."

"Can't have that. A lovely view it is."

"And we need to see this little whipper snipper win in two weeks, got a reputation to maintain."

"No Mon, it was definitely three weeks I'm sure..."

"I'm sorry what?" I started out of my frozen state.

"The hunt, the hunt dear girl! Goodness, you're taking part in the team tryouts; you'd think you'd know when it is."

"When did you hear that?" I ask, voice urgent.

"This morning wasn't it Cleo?" Tutankamon settled back down leaving the way free.

"What exactly did they say? Did they give a date?" I pressed, jostled on all sides as students rushed passed to freedom.

"Well if you calculate the time between now and then," began Cleo.

"By Kelt rotations is best-"

"No! Moons is by far the most accurate-"

"A date!" I fair shouted. "Please just give me a date."

Cleo sat up her expression affronted. "No need to be snappy." Her agitated tail cracked loudly against the stone of the castle.

Tutankamon's brow creased into a thoughtful frown. "The eighth day of High Autumn," he announced proudly, ducking his head down to eye level. "It's our reputation you hold in your little flesh hands. Don't mess it up." He tapped a sharp claw on the steps with every word.

~ Priori

THE IMPORTANCE OF BETA READERS

Sometimes I wish I could download my favourite authors' brains. Imagine all the extra things they'd know about my favourite stories, my favourite characters. Imagine suddenly understanding all the subplots and undercurrents I had missed because I'd been too thick. It's one of the reasons why I became a writer in the first place, because I know *everything* about my world and characters, everything said out loud or implied, I understand the reason behind every action, the way the world operates, why I put things in order A rather than order XXX. It's an additional, enriching experience you can't get being the reader. Of course, you being the only person who knows how your brain puts things together can be a massive problem. Because you don't realise that you haven't put the connections that are in your head onto paper.

A writer may know everything, but if what you know doesn't appear on the page, then how is the reader going to follow your logic? What the writer knows, the reader must know, and sometimes it's hard to separate what you've actually said in black and white from what your brain is filling in for you. The problem is that unless these gaps in knowledge are pointed out to you, it is almost impossible to see them yourself. You know *too* much. It's the one time where being a know-it-all is not in your favour.

Which is why it is essential that you pry loose your death grip on your manuscript, and hand it to someone else to read. This someone else is called your Beta Reader. Beta Readers are an essential part of any editorial journey, they spot the gaps, they make you think about *why* you made something the way you did, and they help you turn your book from a pretty, fuzzy picture into a clear photograph.

In this section I'm going to go through how to pick and train a Beta Reader to give you the feedback you need, and some of the most common 'holes' writers have lurking in their drafts (which you still probably won't be able to find in your own work, but at least you know what they are!).

1: How to Pick a Beta Reader

It's hard to let go of your baby, so picking a helpful Beta Reader is key. You want someone who doesn't just tell you it's great, you need someone who is constructive and is going to tell you what they don't understand or like. Generally you should send it to three or four Beta Readers so that you know the comments are balanced. So what should you look for in a Beta Reader?

- Someone who is NOT part of your family. Unless they are an editor, they won't be objective.

- Pick someone you know is going to be objective and critical (but not try to tear you a new one). This person can be a friend, but again they have to be a friend who likes what you write and isn't afraid to tell you what they think. If they come back to you with no comments on things to change, that does not mean you are the most awesome writer on the planet, it means you picked the wrong person to read. Pass Go, try again.

- In saying that you're not after someone that will tell you you're a horrible writer. They should not be attacking you as the writer, they should be dissecting the story and offering thoughts as to how things can be remedied.

- They must read voraciously in your genre. If they don't understand the basic concepts of mages, witchcraft, wizards, dragons, elves, orcs, or flying houses in the sky, then it's best you don't give that person your manuscript about a fantastical floating island where people fight to the death on Magic Carpets. They're not going to get it. In saying that, a non-genre reader who is also a writer may be better at picking up logic flaws, but you will need to be careful to filter their responses into useful/non-useful based on their lack of understanding.

- Someone who has the time and is a quick reader. You may have someone who is perfect, but if they don't have the time to read and critique, or they take two months to read one book, then they aren't going to be your best pick.

2: How to Train a Beta Reader

Most people you find to read your manuscript aren't going to be trained in the art of Beta Reading. Therefore giving them guidelines will help you get what you need, and will give them an idea of what they're looking for. There are also certain tricks that will make it easier for you to get specific feedback rather than general feedback:

- Provide the manuscript (MS) to them in Word format. You want them to make notes exactly where the confusion arose. Providing them with your MS in PDF or ebook formats will not allow them to do this easily (or for you to access the comments easily). Doing it direct into the word processor is essential.

- Get your Beta to use Track Changes in Word so that you can see where their questions/comments are.

- Provide them with a brief of what you want them to look for. Are there particular things you are worried about? Pacing, characterisation, plot, believability etc.

- Ask them to acknowledge their biases. e.g. They may, as a reader, be more concerned with characterisation, or not be good at spelling, or not read a particular sub-genre very often, or they may dislike particular types of characters in books. If you get them to acknowledge all of this upfront, that will help you judge how much of their feedback to take on board.

- You want them to make *specific* and *overview* comments:

  ○ **Overview comments:** When they finish the novel you want them to give you an overall impression of it. Key things to ask would be: how did you feel at the end? Was there any point where you think things went too slow or didn't fit with the rest? Are there sections you would switch the order of, or extra scenes you wish were included? Or scenes they didn't understand *why* they were included? Were the characters' personalities clear? If not, which ones and what do you *think* the author was trying to make them like? Did you understand each main character's motivation/ intentions?

- Specific Comments: You want them to make comments within the text when: they don't understand something; they need more background information; when you have been contradictory; when they want to know why a character did a particular thing (this means you haven't conveyed their motivations clearly enough); they had to read a line more than once to understand what you were saying (means your sentence is awkward/

convoluted and needs rephrasing); when something seems too easy/ glossed over/coincidental. Another valuable thing to get your readers to do is highlight any points where they feel you are expecting them to work something out but they feel something is missing that stops them doing this. Or any point where you are giving them *too much* information and spoiling the fun of putting the pieces together overtime.

- If your Beta Reader sees a typo or tense change let them know they are free to mark it, *however,* proof reading is not the main job of a Beta. You need to stress that their main focus should be the overview and specific comments.

- Get them to provide examples to help illustrate their point, or have them offer suggestions as to what they think might fix it. Being told something needs to be changed but not *how* can be infuriating for you and anti-productive.

Now that you have some idea of what you are looking for in a Beta Reader, and what your Beta should be looking for in your manuscript, let's move onto some of the common 'holes' in a manuscript that leave a reader scratching their head.

3: Common 'Holes'

A) Not Showing Character Motivation

Readers won't take things on faith, they need reasons, motivation and back story. We have the 'Show don't tell' mantra drilled into us so often that sometimes we go too far the other way. Body language is sometimes not enough, a shrug for one character may mean 'meh' where as a shrug for another character may mean 'I'm going to hide in a closet and scare you when you sleep'. In the examples below you see the need not only to expand upon body language, but also to give background information to a character's reaction.

Accenting the 'dangerous' she looked him straight in the eye. She stared him down for several seconds. He swallowed, then his shoulders slumped.
"All right," he said resigned.

~ Priori – Draft

"Why does he swallow? Is he afraid of her or uneasy about her? That is the implication."

~ Isobelle Carmody

Accenting the 'dangerous' she looked him straight in the eye. He stared her down for several seconds then swallowed, his shoulders slumping. She was just too unpredictable. "Alright."

~ Priori – Rewrite

*

Never before had a building so fascinated my attention.

~ Priori – Draft

"Because ... it was under the earth? Because it was so different to anything she had seen on the surface? Because she knows what it contains? Because it does not look as she imagined? Because of its complexity?"

~ Isobelle Carmody

Never before had a building so fascinated my attention, a new complexity revealing itself in every pass.

~ Priori – Rewrite

B) Contradictions

It's inevitable, when writing an 80,000 word MS over the course of twelve months, that you are going to forget some vital piece of character background or minor superpower that you bestowed on your hero. In *Priori*, one of Beverly's minor gifts, being able to talk to animals, became not so minor when she is attacked by a 'Razorfin' (yes, it's just an obnoxious name for 'Shark)'. In the original draft I was so caught up in creating drama that I conveniently ignored the fact that she should have been able to talk to said razorfin about *not* eating her. An entire scene suddenly needed rethinking when Isobelle said:

> *"Can't she talk to animals because of the Priori?"*

> ~ Isobelle Carmody

Bugger. Yes. Back to the drawing board.

C) You've Only Done Vague World Building

Whether you intricately plot your novel, or start with only an idea, when you write the first draft you're just trying to get the basic order of events down on a page, like a sculptor attacking a piece of marble with a jackhammer. The subtlety comes later in revision, and with each editing pass the holes get smaller. But sometimes there is a throwaway line that trips up a reader, or an inconsistency that they jump on about the history of your world that you haven't explicitly described. The first example, the throwaway line is normally an easy fix, but the second example requires more thought. With histories you have to be careful not to info-dump on your readers and will need to weave and hint at the history throughout your novel:

A look of pure greed lit the unkempt faces of the two soldiers, for a rich reward came with our capture.

~ Priori – Draft

"What is the reward for? People trying to escape the testing or her specifically (the host)? In which case does the soldier know of the Priori/ her power? I think he needs to say something more specific that makes it clear the reward is for her specifically."

~ Isobelle Carmody

*

My first testing was on my twelfth birthday and since then I have had many more, too many to count. Once a month a loud knock on the door signals their presence as the Ruhle army heft a heavy machine into the house.

~ Priori – Draft

"Why are children being tested over and over? Surely a single test would reveal that a child is not the Host, unless they know of the stolen sholac and guess its use, or unless the power will enter only when it chooses, so kids have to be tested over and over."

~ Isobelle Carmody

I knew why the children were continually tested, but to show that required the dropping of clues as well as the invention of an entirely new scene. I hadn't thought the information mattered, but clearly for a reader to trust me as a storyteller they had to know I wasn't just 'inventing' plot points. Ironic.

D) Shit Doesn't Just Happen, People Discuss Things

At times you want to rush through all the boring 'admin' scenes to get to the action. *You* know all that has gone on, but for a reader, not seeing a discussion and just having things 'work out' is a little convenient, as you can see in Isobelle's comments below.

Elitree gestured to two chutes, one for each of us. With a wave Charlie stood under his hole and disappeared.

~ Priori – Draft

"This is too expedient – the Master must say a few words. At the beginning he needs to make clear what he makes of her and what is to happen, and this should be a reminder. It is all very well that he is magic and knows all, but we don't. We need to see that mundane natural conversation, it need not be more than the odd sentence, but make it a good sentence. For instance, he does not tell them where they are going before Charlie is dispatched."

~ Isobelle Carmody

As I said, these four 'hole' types can be very hard to spot in your own manuscript, hence the need for a select Beta Reading Army Of Awesome. You will come back to these readers again and again as you build your writing career. Treat them well and they will be a reliable part of your editing plan in the future.

Exercise

This is less an exercise and more a preparation for the

---

future when you will have need of a good network of Beta Readers.

- **Step 1:** List on a piece of paper all of the people you know who fit the Beta Reading criteria in this chapter. i.e. they are not family, they are objective and critical (but not in a mean way, in a constructive way), they read in your genre, they have the time and are quick to give feedback. Sometimes you won't know their suitability in the final criteria until you approach them.

- **Step 2:** Contact each of those people asking them if they would be willing to beta read a short story or two to three chapters for you. Their response to your request (and subsequent comments on your MS) will tell you if they are a suitable beta reader for your style of writing.

- **Step 3:** If you *don't* have more than two or three names on your list, you need to explore ways to network with other writers who can help. Google search for writers groups in your area, or online writers groups that you can share your writing with. In exchange you will need to read and comment on their writing, in fact you should offer to do this *first*, before your own draft is complete. This system only works if you are willing to be as giving as others. Be respectful of your writing group members and they *should* afford you the same respect in return.

In the below Golden Moment you'll see the beginnings of character motivation, which turns into a scene where the young woman, Satinay, 'discusses' her seemingly impulsive plan to rescue the main character, Beverly, from the perils of the surface with her brother. It makes the conversation that follows much more dynamic as a result.

Golden Moments

The woman in the mirror nodded curtly and was gone, her image replaced by the man's tense, reflected face.

Hiding behind an alcove at the back of the room was a young woman of eighteen. Midnight black hair framed her unusually pale-skinned face, and highlighted her mischievous ice blue eyes.

During the secret exchange between her father and his operative, her mind had formed the beginnings of a plan. One that, if successful, would cause her father to take her desire to join his sector seriously.

~ Priori

ENDINGS

Endings are harder than you think. Or they should be if you're doing it right. There's a tendency in genre writing to go for the easiest fix, the ending that proves black is black and white is white, and if you're writing epic fantasy, that danger looms on the horizon with ten thousand sharp teeth and a PMS problem. Endings are as important as beginnings; if you leave the reader with a clichéd trope the chances of them singing your praises is about as likely as your ability to spontaneously morph into a mermaid. John Cleese did an amazing speech on creativity in which he encouraged creatives to play with endings long after they had happened upon the most obvious one; to have fun with the generation of ideas rather than treating it like work. He would sometimes play with the endings of his Monty Python sketches for hours past the most obvious joke. By playing with these ideas he would come across the most surprising and funny conclusions.

It was through the generation of such original ideas that Monty Python found success, and it is a sentiment I've taken to heart, particularly ever since I wrote my first choose your own adventure story as part of my Story City project (which Isobelle has also written an adventure for in Brisbane). For my story, a real-life choose your own adventure through the streets of Adelaide, South Australia, I had to create eight different endings. It was one of the hardest writing 'exercises' I had ever set myself, because once the obvious two to three endings had been penned, I still had to find another five endings that would leave a reader satisfied (or righteously pissed off because I'd 'killed' them with an alien ray-gun).

While I won't pretend it didn't take hours of blankly staring at walls and suddenly interrupting conversations with, "What if the unicorn in the building façade suddenly came to life and impaled the spaceship with his horn?" I did find that the endings I was most proud of were those last five, pulled from the ether and satisfyingly mashed together. If I were to make a linear narrative and pick one path for the reader, I would end it with one of those last, rather desperately created, story ideas. Because overall they were the most original, surprising, and true.

Endings in novels come in two types, the ending of the novel and story arc as a whole, and the ending of chapters. Each has a different purpose. I have never had trouble writing chapter endings, as I've read enough good (and bad) books to know what makes me want to give up hours of precious sleep. See if you can spot why Isobelle, my writing mentor, was so excited by the below chapter endings:

With a sigh, the boy checked he had his dagger in his boot and the straps of his pack were securely tightened. If they were going to the surface to find the child with the Priori, he wanted to make sure he was ready for everything. He knew who would get blamed if his sister was hurt or if they led the Ruhle to the Priori. He moved to his sister's side and together they took a deep breath, pushing their way into the centre of the liquid sphere. After a slight pause they slowly shimmered out of existence in an explosion of coloured lights.

~ Priori

"Great end of chapter!"

~ Isobelle Carmody

*

I had such a feeling of déjà vu that I didn't react until it was too late. Shima reared in terror. My breath caught in my throat as the ball slammed into my chest, my body absorbing the blue energy as the impact launched me off Shima's back and into the air. My last memory was of screams, as thousands of tonnes of earth and rock descended from the roof.

~ Priori

"Wow exciting end!"

~ Isobelle Carmody

Each chapter ending is a cliff hanger, an exciting, suspenseful discovery, or event that leaves the reader struggling to put the book down. These must be carefully crafted for each chapter and generally leave a strong visual image. A visual is a way to reinforce intrigue, mystery and suspense, making it visceral as well as intellectual. You can double the effect by naming the chapter after with an intriguing or unexpected title, which is what I do for my Grand Adventures of Madeline Cain book series. Your aim with chapter endings is to make sure the reader can't put your book down until they've reached the last page.

The ending of a novel is a different beast all together. As I mentioned previously, the best endings involve a lot of playing with ideas before a writer actually commits themselves to the final path. The ending of a novel needs to tie up subplots, concluding the sidekick's love affair with a turtle, or the protagonist's daddy issues, or the impact of the hero's actions on that town they accidentally set on fire etc etc. It also needs to examine the emotional impact on the character. How different are they from the start of the book when they began their journey? Because the mystery(s) has been solved, and the exciting events are in the past, this is where many fantasy authors find themselves falling into cliché, like I did at the end of the first draft for *Priori*:

Yes the Kraken was still out there and yes I would face him again. But then there was nothing I could do about it; no way I could avoid it. What was it the Brethren had said? Oh, yes. <u>Destiny cannot be sought but faced with grace. All I can hope is that I can face such a destiny.</u>

~ Priori – Draft

"This does not seem to strive high enough for the very end statement in a story. Try to find some different words, ones that don't feel like a cliché from a dozen interchangeable fantasy novels. Strive for the truth of this moment. How would you feel? What would you think? Try to find an original sentiment and words to express it."

~Isobelle Carmody

I smiled. Charlie, still trying to guide his little sister from afar. Yes the Kraken was still out there and yes I would face him again. But then there was nothing I could do about it; no way I could avoid it. The time for hiding was over; it was time to face things as Charlie would, with courage.

~ Priori – Rewrite

The rewrite for the end of *Priori* was much more in keeping with the relationship between the main character Beverly and her brother Charlie, referring to the sentiment in a previous scene. Being able to express emotions in a true, non-cliché way, relies on you knowing your character well. You need to know their motivations, their connections to other characters in the book and how the actions of others have impacted your protagonist's original state of mind. This requires you to keep track of their emotional arc. This is where having 'deep and meaningfuls' with friends can help (yes that includes you gents, get your D&Ms on). These D&M conversations are how writers can observe the reactions, feelings and emotions of different people. Two people will not react in the same way to the same situation. Collecting these reactions and folding them into your characters, will give you the emotional resonance you need to avoid cliché.

You'll also notice that the above ending sets up a further mystery, as this is the first book in a planned series. The reason why this mystery isn't turned into a cliff hanger, as you would the ending of a chapter, is because I don't know when I will get to writing the next book. There is no better way to piss off your readers than to leave them hanging at the end of a three hundred page book and take a year or two to write the next one. If you want your readers salivating for the next book, then by all means leave a large dangling taunt at the end. Just be ready for the onslaught of reader pressure until you get the next in the series out of the labyrinth that is your creative mind.

Exercise

Let's get a handle on the whole endings thing by returning to the examination of your favourite book.

- Step 1: Make a pros and cons list about what is good/bad about the ending of the current book you're reading by another author. Did it leave you hanging? Did it miss out important characters? Or did it do all those things right? Really analyse what makes that ending great or where the possible room for improvement is.

- Step 2: Using dot points, plot out a new, and different ending for this book. The dot points might detail things such as:

    ○ If it's set in a different setting,

    ○ If the character uses a different method to fight,

    ○ Or a new angle or solution to win,

    ○ If secondary characters have a

greater hand in the outcome,

- ○ If someone who gave them a key piece of information never existed and how that changed the outcome etc.

- Step 3: Then make yourself a list of how your ending fixes the cons in the pros and cons list you made.

- Step 4: Now, the next time you plot (or maybe rewrite) your novel, allow yourself time to imagine at least half a dozen alternate endings. Might I recommend doing this in mind-map form, where the centre is a particular point near the end of the book. Then the branches going off the mind map are the different directions the ending could take. There might be more or less help from secondary characters. You might have one person play a bigger role. Or different external factors affect the outcome: world events, weather, the arrival of help or the rearranging of an 'aha' moment etc. You may surprise yourself with the twists you can come up with!

Golden Moments

Barely a second later came the muffled sound of footsteps. My sword was in my hand before Charlie even heard a noise. Not again, I thought, taking a wide fighting stance. There must be hundreds of them searching for us.

~ Priori

"This is a good chapter ending. Suspenseful and exciting."

~ Isobelle Carmody

Deepen The Story

DEEPEN THE STORY

I tend to compare the first draft of a story to a 70,000 word pool of Tweets. You started off with maybe ten big ideas, which turned into 20 minor ideas which you then cobble together into the essence or skeleton of a story. There are times when you know a scene in great detail and other times when you just say something happened to get to the part that you know. The problem with tweets and even with 7,000 tweets strung together, (at ten words a tweet) is that you don't know what the whole of it looks like until it's done. Which ultimately results in a story with a lot of action (by that I mean movement rather than the genre) but not a lot of substance. A lot of clichés, but lacking a little in originality. If this doesn't describe your work after the first or even third draft, I hate you. Gift me part of your supercomputer brain.

The main bulk of my mentorship with Isobelle wound

up being a yearlong lesson in originality, in delving into the motivations behind a character's action, behind a coincidence, and in essence, deepening a story so it looks like a canyon rather than a blue line on a map. This may not be true for other writers, but what I tend to see in my head when I write are scenes, which means my first drafts are full of description and fast paced action. I had always thought, 'action is dramatic, I've got drama coming out of my ears.' However, you should never mistake action for drama or action for emotional growth of a character. Novels and stories thrive on conflict and action is only the physical component of that. You shouldn't limit your narrative ups and downs to major physical events or scenes, but make sure every physical event has a series of little ups and downs, belief and disbelief, try and fail and try again. Because let's face it, if our protagonist gets it right the first time, why would you bother to tell the story? Or read it?

There are three main categories that Isobelle's *I think you could deepen this* comments seemed to fall into. When I read my second drafts now I always do a special read through to identify these sorts of scenes.

1: Coincidences & Good 'Luck'

Pushing himself gingerly to his feet he reached out to part the vines revealing a hidden cave. A natural maze of moss-covered boulders had made it difficult to look anywhere but where we were going. If he had not fallen at that exact spot we would never have stumbled upon the hide-a-way.

~ Priori – Draft

"Feels a little convenient, but maybe it was not a coincidence that he fell..."

~ Isobelle Carmody

It was such a little comment, but it was the first time I realised there is no such thing as coincidence in a good story. We build these conveniences into a first draft because we want to get to the bit that we know, but the second draft is the time to expand on these 'place holders'. In the original draft this was the only explanation I had about how they found this cave. But I was missing out on a chance not only to world build but cement and demonstrate the difference between Beverly and her brother. Below is the rewrite, a bit more dynamic, no?

Thump! I started violently, twisting in the saddle then smothered a near hysterical snort with one hand. Behind me a quivering tree branch had swept Charlie off Comet's back and proceeded to shed drops of water over him.

Dismounting, I reached my hand out to my silently swearing brother. I cocked my head to the side as I looked at the branch. "How bizarre. I could have sworn that wasn't there when I passed by a moment ago."

"Oh it's there," Charlie affirmed as I pulled him to his feet with a grunt.

I stumbled and fell against the cliff wall only to feel it give way. I turned to the fall of vines which hung along the cliff face and put my hand through a gap in the foliage. "Well, would you look at that," I breathed, putting my other hand through and parting the tendrils. "A cave!"

Eyes straining to see in the dark, Charlie moved closer. "What have you been smoking? It's just hard rock. Come on, we have to find a place to rest before the hunting parties catch up."

"What are you talking about?" I almost cried. I forced my voice to a whisper, "It's right there." I grabbed his arm and heard a hiss. My head snapped around to the boulder strewn landscape, searching for movement.

"It was just rock. Then you touched me and... and it was gone!" He stared at the cavern thoughtfully. "Let go of my arm."

I peeled my fingers from his bicep, ashamed of my knee-jerk reaction.

"And now the stone's back." Charlie leant forward and ran a hand along the air behind the vines. "I can feel it, it's rough and wet and cold. Touch me again."

Perplexed I obliged. Charlie's hand jerked back then reached right through, nothing impeding his fingers.

"Marvellous, some sort of energy is hiding the cave. I think we've found our hideaway for the night. Don't let go, I don't want to be stuck half way through a rock wall."

"Mmmm, uncomfortable," I whispered back.

~ Priori – Rewrite

2: No One Gets it Right the First Time – Little Ups & Downs

Magick in the *Priori* is accessed via a type of relic, a medallion that is keyed to a specific person. It acts as a focusing tool to see the Lines of Power, a grid of invisible magick that is used for most spells. In the example below, Beverly, the main character, had only learnt about the Lines of Power's existence six hours earlier.

"That's not an option," I replied. With my hand over my medallion I tweaked a Line of Power lifting both to their feet as Satinay had shown me the previous night.

~ Priori – Draft

"Here is a great opportunity to develop and detail your story – we should see her try and fail and try to do this – it is too easy if she just gets it."

~ Isobelle Carmody

This was originally a throwaway line, something to show the magick now in the Beverly's life, the day after she learnt about her power. Basically, a lazy bit of world building. However, you should never give up the opportunity to create a little drama, to add a trill of minor ups and downs that not only cause tension and added colour, but actually help your character develop emotionally. As Isobelle said, it's too easy if she gets it, and let's face it, *no one* gets it right the first time, not in Storyland.

Another one of Isobelle's deepening questions earlier in the manuscript asked how Beverly felt about her power, and asked whether she knew it could be used to destroy and whether she had used it for anything else. It got me thinking about the character's emotional arc, her inner story, and I realised that at the beginning she had no evidence to suggest that her power could do anything other than destroy. She didn't have enough control over it. But because she didn't know any better, she believed it was the power that was wild, not that her control was lacking.

This throwaway line had the potential to become its own scene, to create drama and explore Beverly's emotional growth. This is the scene that developed from those two sentences.

I just stared at it. "But what if I can't see them? What if killing people and destroying sheds is all the Priori can do? All I can do?" I asked in a small voice.

"You can only try," replied Charlie.

"At the very least, prove us wrong," quipped Cypress.

I reached out, my fingers hovering over the medallion as though *it would burn me. Before I could change my mind, I snatched it from Satinay's hand. In my palm, it pulsed red. There was an answering burst of light from the sword. I touched the stone with my thumb and both dimmed.*

Something flickered at the edge of my vision. I looked up. Before me, spread in every direction, were straight silver threads, a grid of Lines that ran through the space, into the cavern walls and even through Charlie and the twins. "I can see them," I breathed in wonder. A Line lit up as I touched it.

"Try to use them, like Satinay did," urged Cypress. "Focus on the Line you want and trace it up, you don't have to be touching it."

Hesitating, I reached out for one that stretched from floor to ceiling, through one of the hessian bags. But the thread stayed dormant. "It's not working!"

"Don't panic," ordered Satinay, closing my fingers back over the medallion. "There's one more thing you have to do when you trace the Line. You need to imagine there's a little bit of the Priori in the tip of your finger, alright."

"Calling the Priori is not a good idea," I moaned.

"Just a pinprick. Don't call anything, just imagine it's there. Ok?"

Mutely, I nodded. A vision of the Priori appeared in my head in an instant and I clamped down on it hard, shrinking the image down until it was so small I could barely see it. I imagined it resting on my finger tip. Opening my eyes I reached for the same Line as before. It flared to life. My finger jerked, and the bag lurched to one side.

"It moved!" I cried.

~ Priori – Rewrite

3: Motivations & Changes of Pace

In the below example I had not truly thought through the motivations for Beverly's reactions and how that affected the emotional pace of the narrative.

"Look, Bluebell," Charlie pressed steady hands against the wooden grain, fingertips turning white. "I don't want to overstay my welcome. Elitree has been very kind to me. I feel I have to go out on my own for a while. You'll be fine...you always have been."

Stubbornly I persisted, "You should have discussed it with me. We should have discussed it. We, who have lived together our whole lives. We, who kept the secret. We, who kept each other sane. We, who- "

"Me! Whose whole life has revolved around his sister! Her secret, her safety!" his voice snapped out like a whip, hands pounding once against the hard wood. Looks of guilt and determination warred upon his features.

Frozen to the spot I could not respond. He rubbed a hand over his eyes. "Listen I have to tie up some loose ends. I'll meet you near the front steps of the Academy tomorrow morning." Charlie shot one last worried glance and strode out the door.

I slammed my notebook shut.

"Hey! Where you going?"

"Sword practise. Are you coming, Cypress?" I stalked out, seething at my brother's inability to tell me anything before it was too late to talk.

Original Fantasy

~ Priori – Draft

"I was expecting her to dwell on this a little, acknowledge that his words are fair enough, but it does not happen, she goes back to reproaching him for his lack of notice, it seems a bit thoughtless and unfair. It might be nice to have a deeper conversation between them to give us a break from the endless banter and side remarks of the characters to one another; it might be good to introduce the odd change of pace from time to time."

~ Isobelle Carmody

I had clung to that lazy excuse that she reacted as she did because of an age old annoyance with her brother's personality. But so much upheaval had gone on in the lives of these two characters, frankly, I could come up with a better reason than a childish annoyance.

In life, we all tell ourselves these excuses, but in reality we just don't know how to articulate the raw feelings. As a writer, it was my *job* to articulate them. In the original manuscript this scene was followed up with Beverly sulking, then accepting that that's how her brother was, seeing how happy he was and deciding to forgive him, all internally without a meaningful conversation between them. There was no emotional growth, no drama, and no exploration of the subconscious reasons. So I added a later conversation as Isobelle suggested, that explored the motivation behind Beverly's reaction and changed the pace and focus for a little while.

I suddenly recalled all those times I had seen him in the hall alone as I hurried from task to task, his eyes searching the crowd and lighting up when he spotted me. Now that I thought about it, his search had a kind of desperation about it, his arms crossed protectively across his chest, his shoulders set in a despondent slouch. How often had I made time for him in these past few months? A dozen times? The realisation hit me like a blow to the stomach. Who had abandoned who first?

Heaving myself to my feet, I moved towards Charlie's voice in the back room determined to set things right. "I'm sorry," I blurted, bursting into the room. "I'm sorry I didn't pay enough attention, I'm sorry I didn't realise how you were feeling."

Charlie stood half bent by a box, his back to me. Voice thick he said, "When I realised you didn't need my help anymore, I just felt lost."

"Why didn't you say anything?"

"You've never had a life Bev, not a normal one. It's been so wonderful to see you come alive here, I didn't want to ruin that with my problems."

"No, we are a team," I insisted, "You looked after me all this time and when it was my turn to pay you back, I choked. I want you to have all the joy I have."

He turned, opening his arms. I rushed into them. He rubbed my back and murmured, "Thank you. And I will; you're safe and my new job has given me a purpose. This move has already shown me I have more friends than I knew. I just had to let go a little to realise that. I'm standing on my own feet, and in time the Circle of

Magick will realise that I can do more than advise. They'll see that the magick does make the person. But I'll be here for everything you do, whenever you need me."

"I know," I whispered.

~ Priori – Rewrite

Exercise

Deepening the story not only allows the reader to get to know a character or world more fully, but it also allows you to add drama, conflict and motivation to your narrative. The best way to get the hang of this is to practice!

Part 1

- Step 1: Grab the most recent fiction book you've been reading. Find one of these throw away lines, lines that could have sprung a whole scene of intrigue.

- Step 2: Now write the scene you think could have sprung from that line, keeping in mind those three 'deepening' categories: avoid coincidence, you never get it right the first time, and what's the motivation.

- Step 3: Do the same thing for a different book by a different author. Doing this more than once allows you to identify these opportunities more easily in your own work.

Part 2

- Step 1: Now look for at least three of these potential lines that can turn into a scene in your manuscript.

- Step 2: Rewrite the one with the most potential as your next writing exercise.

In the Golden Moment Isobelle highlighted below, we break from the regular first person narrative (this is done about 5-6 times during the novel) to dive deeper into the story of the people who live in the safe haven of Creana. This way the reader can see they have as many worries and hopes and dreams as the main character who is seeking refuge there.

Golden Moments

A tall man sat facing her, his face was pale and his deep black hair was gathered into a ponytail at the nape of his neck.

His white knuckled hand gripped the arm of his chair. "The first sighting in eighteen years," he breathed, his mind immediately contemplating multiple courses of action.

~ Priori

THE PROBLEM OF EVIL

I always ran, hoping I'd outrun the evil. The one that was going to swallow me if I couldn't get out of its sight.

~ Beverly Jordan, Priori – Draft

Evil. It's a pretty problematic word in fantasy because it's overused. More often than not it's used because the writer can't be bothered explaining clearly or threw it in there for a little drama. There is a mentality in fantasy that you don't need to explain evil, everyone knows what evil is right? Guy who organises genocide – Evil. Guy who murders a man to marry his wife – Evil. Guy who steals food and a tellie from a poor family of ten – Evil. Guy who kicks over a sandcastle a little girl spent three hours building – Evil. Channel Ten cancelling Castle for a football game – Evil. Ah yes, now we begin to see that not all evils are equal... The world is not all black and white my young Jedi for there are shades of evil and each reader has a different definition.

Evil has become a blanket term or a label, like 'good' or 'heroic' which is often merely a way for the writer to not have to explain *why* the person is good or heroic. Why is it evil, how did it get there, how do you notice it, how does it affect people, is it worse at different times, why is it worse, what gets evil's goat, why does it cut their façade? In the above line from an old *Priori* draft I threw in a vague feeling, without explaining what the evil was, how it manifested, or why it would bother to swallow her whole. For a good writer the answer is *never*, "That's just what it does. It's evil man!" If you use such a word, be careful to use it in an explicit way, such as the change I made below.

I always ran, hoping I'd outrun the evil. That menacing shade that made the villagers secretive and dampened the spirit of every adult I'd ever met. The one that was going to swallow me whole like it had them, leaving only an echo of who I was if I couldn't get out of its sight.

~ Beverly Jordan, Priori – Rewrite

The way you can usurp these labels by giving your 'evil' character, or 'heroic' character, or 'good' character a backstory, fleshing the out so that they are real, not archetypal. Chances are most of this backstory won't make it into your novel, but you will be able to use it to make sure the character's actions and reactions ring true to their background.

You need to be aware that these labels, this crutch of overused terms exists and you need to be strong enough to throw it away and walk on your own two feet to get the great story.

Exercise

Evil can mean different things to different people. Each character will have their own Scale of Bad. To someone who has been wealthy all their life, a thief who steals from a market place is evil. To someone who has had to work hard to get to a wealthy position, the need to steal may be understandable, but the casual cruelty of a politician to the starving population is evil.

In the exercise below pick three or four types of characters and describe what the tipping point of evil is for these characters, from their point of view. Preferably pick ones that match characters already in your manuscript. Or feel free to add to the list different types of people that may be more relevant to your genre, whatever works for you at this point of your writing journey. Was there an event that tipped them over the edge? What role did belief play in their transformation etc?

A street urchin; a milk maid; a hero; a farmer; a merchant man; a mage; a prince; a bastard prince; a foot soldier; a privileged knight; a teacher; a scientist; a president; a human rights activist; an environmentalist; a tradesperson (known in Australia as a 'tradie'); an apocalypse survivor; a factory worker; a single mother on minimum wage; natural disaster victim; a child soldier; a mother; an activist; a police officer/detective

In the Golden Moment below, Beverly's antagonist, the Kraken, has sent a message in the form of her mother, mind wiped, and a vessel for his words. The scene around this moment doesn't show him as evil, more cold, calculating and with a clear ability to invoke hysteria which gives him the upper hand in his plan. He is a personality that you see in life, not a one-D person who's just out there to 'mess shit up'.

Golden Moments

When she spoke her voice was deeper, that of a man's, hard and triumphant. Her hand squeezed my arm, clenching tighter with each word. "You did not think you could hide forever?"

~ Priori

THE NAMING OF THINGS

I've quoted the start of a favourite book of mine several times in this book:

> *"But names are important!" the nursemaid protested.*
> *"Yes," said Quillam Mye. "So is accuracy."*

~ Fly by Night, Frances Hardinge

This quote really hits it on the head – names *are* important. The number of fantasy books that cite the 'power of a true name' are too numerous to count (if that law of magic were at play in our world, I'd probably use it for evil... mmm, foot rubs for life). This notion has to have come from somewhere and that somewhere is probably the author being told by an editor to *make it count*.

Names can't just sound good, or look impressive, they need to fit, and in fiction, they need to have meaning. Just as there is no such thing as coincidence in fiction (you try it and your readers may well lynch mob you) there is no such thing as a name that means nothing. As stated above, they need accuracy to them. Names are analysed for hidden meaning by readers, so you may as well make yourself look clever.

I'm not talking so much about giving your characters meaningful names, but more about giving things, races, places and activities names with a bit more thought than what glee you'll have being the only human able to pronounce them. For example, the naming of my blog (and hence this book) was quite important, as you will have read in the first chapter.

There are two facets of naming you need to consider:

1: The Proper Two Hour Ponder

As mentioned above, the naming of things, races, places and activities with a little more thought than honouring your neighbour's best friend's dog is essential in any genre, but particularly in fantasy. The whole genre is a thoughtless trip hazard, overly long names and pretty words strewn about like an obstacle course. I want to imprison in a sound proof bubble thoughtless authors who name their main character Charhelthbalthazar and then complain that the fantasy genre doesn't get the audience it deserves. It's because you're bashing readers upside the head with that spiky club of a name; seriously, calling her Cindy is only going to raise the bar in your story.

My initial drafts of *Priori* seemed to be balanced between thoughtful naming and slap dash 'that will do' words as caught by Isobelle's eagle eye below:

"The different stones represent the three guilds. Opal is the gem for Cosmica; the Sapphire is the gem for Mistico, and the Ruby is the gem for Firefre guild." Cypress indicated the various stones as he spoke. "Each guild has a different responsibility within the city."

~ Priori – Draft

"What do these names mean? They don't grab me at the moment. Any reason you didn't use 'real' words? You have to be careful when you invent words. This is what puts a lot of people off a fantasy at first glance. So if you use them they have to be good – it can't be to establish your imagined world as you are doing that quite well – the Priori is a good name, the Ruhle Army is good, the dwarf's name, Olimpan, is unusual and unique but somehow real sounding – but these three feel a bit new-age-y and also hastily contrived, but as I said if you have good reasons for them, that will eventually resonate and they can grow on a reader."

~ Isobelle Carmody

Yeah, I only had a good reason for one of those; I think the other two were a 'for the hell of it' kind of naming. The three guilds are now called Aeri (for the weather workers), Glasuna (for those who work with the glass dome) and Firefre (for those who work with the spheres of light) to better reflect what each guild actually does. In *Priori*, the best example of a name that was meaningful and chosen carefully is 'Alaequine', basically a winged horse or Pegasus. I smooshed two Latin words together, 'ala'- meaning winged and 'equine' obviously meaning horse.

2: World Lingo

By this I mean how the characters name and refer to themselves in the story (and whether or not it fits into the world you build). Depending on various class distinctions and societal formality, 'respectful' or 'disrespectful' names in each author's world are going to be vastly different. Take the below example from my original *Priori* draft:

Only Fidleton stood her ground, her medallion blazed against the bare skin of her throat.

~ Priori – Draft

"I continue to find the use of names [by the characters] difficult.

Is it possible the teachers could have some sort of honorific, which occasionally the students could drop in their private conversations? Also, I think the students should be addressed by their first names and not their second. It seems odd that Syrrah uses Jordan as a derogative when teachers are regularly addressed by their second names. I think you need to rethink the naming – it is clear you are modelling this on the old English boarding school style as Rowling did with Dumbledore etc. in Harry Potter, but in this text it does not feel right to me. It still seems disrespectful for Beverly to call the Master of the school Elitree, though I like him calling his co-worker her first name in stress."

~ Isobelle Carmody

If I thought about it, I never referred to my school teachers by their last name, it was always prefaced by Ms, Mr, or Mrs (or boring, butt-faced, and crazy if the teen rebellious stage was upon me – and even then only in my head). The teachers always referred to us and each other by first names. I still can't bring myself to call teachers (who I've kept in touch with) by their first name. It's like I've got a short circuit in my brain forever more.

In every society there is a set order of who is higher or lower and while many have done away with bowing, the way we primarily show respect is through our language and naming. I had never thought through the mechanics of that before, it was one of those things where if it was wrong, readers noticed but didn't understand why it felt wrong. For a writer, not getting it right is dangerous, because a reader can take this uncomfortable feeling and misinterpret it as a dislike of the book and abandon it. All my 'teaching' characters now have honorifics that denote their own position in the magical framework of my story: 'Adept' for qualified magick user, 'Enchanter' for advanced magick user, 'Master' for the head of the school etc.

I'll end this section with one final observation. If your book is full of names longer than ten letters, with strange accents and unpronounceable letter groupings, I am going to give up. Too hard, I'm going to play leap frog over those names to get to the parts that don't stop me with their stupidity. Then I'm going to fall back on my default book favourites when I have my next bookish discussion with friends. Because I can't discuss a book with characters whose names I can't pronounce, just like I choose not to talk about anywhere in the Czech Republic other than Prague, anywhere in Norway other than Oslo, anywhere in Iceland other than... nope, nope I can't even discuss the capital because I'm *still* not sure how that is pronounced (Icelanders, you shall have to educate me!), so I just talk about volcanos and Jules Verne instead.

I don't *connect* with characters I can't pronounce easily. Because stupid arse, weirdly spelt names put a massive barrier with an 'F-off' sign between me and the character. There's a reason baby name books exist. Use them.

The below Golden Moment is part of the description

of the underwater city of Creana. And while I could have called those types of trees all kinds of names, I settled on something sensible and easy. Can you guess what I called them? That's correct. I called them Ice Trees. That is their name, no need to complicate things. Simples.

Golden Moments

Several levels were dominated by massive ice-blue trees.

~ Priori

WORLD BUILDING – MAKE BELIEVE IN FIVE QUICK & DIRTY STEPS

There is a myth in fantasy and sci-fi that in order to world build properly you need to create your own personal set of encyclopaedias so large they would flatten an elephant if you dropped them out of a plane. It's the unspoken rule that at least 60% of this encyclopaedia needs to appear in your epic ten volume series. I know it seems like I blame Tolkien for everything, but it really is his fault. I suppose he was a professor of English, so he had to do *something* with his time to justify the paycheque, but ever since the Lord of the Rings became the new 'ultimate standard' we have had a plethora of never ending series of books almost 800 pages long.

World building in some senses is a requirement for all

writers. While the people and places in fiction may be mirrored from real life, you can't guarantee or depend on the idea that a reader is going to be familiar with the lower east side of Manhattan, or the middle of the Australian outback or the gagtastic taste of fried scorpion on a stick in Beijing. Even writers of contemporary reads need to recreate the real places in their fiction, choose key details that are unique and imply a swag of other things that add up to that particular culture.

So while world building is unavoidable for any writer (and a necessity for fantasy and sci-fi writers) there are easy ways to do it and hard ways to do it. You can do the encyclopaedia thing, or you can have a succinct series of question and answer prompts that guide story and character reactions rather than pad your manuscript to look like a literary version of the Michelin Man. Whichever way you choose to create your world, the key is to not let your world building overtake the story like an insidious fungus. You don't want your descriptions to outnumber every other element. At best, you'll have a hard time gathering new fans because they can't get through the meaty chunks where nothing much happens, at worst you'll start losing old fans because they've given up skim reading in their spare time.

If you are someone who likes to build the encyclopaedia of your world before writing, please remember that you *do not* need to force your million pages of world building into the body of the story. Save it, use it as bonus material, interesting blog posts, a new line of toilet paper for hardcore fans. The information should only come out if it's relevant to that particular story line and that particular character. If you find pleasure or use in doing mass amounts of world building, that's fine, but the readers only need the taster platter, not the smorgasbord. Don't tell all your stories in one go, it's how fascinating series are born like Tamora Pierce's Tortall world, Anne McCaffrey's Dragonriders of Pern, or Ursula Le Guin's Earthsea books. Below are my do's and don'ts for world building, my five quick and dirty steps if you will.

1: Do Your Research, Fool

Every awesome fake world is grounded in some way with an interesting real one. There *must* be something familiar for the reader to latch onto, something that taps into their comfort zone of what is *real* and what is not. Readers will connect with the familiar and accept the rest on faith. If there is nothing for them to grasp they will be left floundering, and no reader likes to be made to feel confused or stupid. This is less restricting than you think.

Wanna go Steampunk? Check out the steam crazy Victorian England. Keen for a barbarian horde? Check out ancient Mongolia. Looking for a futuristic landscape where you don't have to touch anything to make it work? Check out modern day Japan. Tap into some of the world's real life mysteries, or ruins and see where fantastical explanations can take you.

2: Ask the Question, Make the Rules

There is nothing more annoying than finding yourself in an alternate reality and half way through the book you realise, anything goes and the conflict is a whole lot of bullshit. 'Well if they could have *thought* themselves a helicopter, why couldn't they *think* themselves out of that dominatrix straightjacket in chapter three?'

Just like real life, fictional worlds operate consistently within a spectrum of physical and societal rules. You just have to figure out what those actually *are*. This is where you do all of the heavy creating which will most likely never make it into the book. One of the first things you have to realise, is you need to start paying attention to every detail you invent, because each event is going to imply things big and small. Is a villager in the centre of a continent eating a fish dinner? Then that's going to imply fast and reliable transport if the character isn't expecting to get food poisoning. If there is a massive sea battle with an invading Viking horde, then you need to be able to come up with a really good reason as to why the village on the water was sacked and pillaged without a fight as a Viking horde would be a natural danger to prepare for in such a village.

This is going to involve you asking and answering a lot of questions to set up a consistent framework for your world. That way when you write your story (which takes place in a tiny portion of your world's history) you know where you are, when you are, and what the characters should know and what their part is in causing the future. I highly recommend checking out Patricia Wrede's list of world building questions on the Science Fiction and Fantasy Writers of America (http://www.sfwa.org/2009/08/fantasy-worldbuilding-questions/) website. They cover everything from the world, physical and historical features, magic rules, people and customs, social organisation, trade and daily life.

3: Don't Make it Awkward – Build Only What You Need, Imply the Rest

There are some things that you're going to invent just to *prove* to everyone (including yourself) that your world is unique. But when you add it to the prose, it stands out like a sore thumb. Take for example my rather clumsy attempt in the first draft of *Priori* below:

Elitree gave an amused smile. "Being awake for... how long is it now?"
"Over 27 hour glasses," I responded.

"There you have it, well over a day. I have no doubt you need sleep."

~ Priori – Draft

"I get it that you are doing this in order to build a world that is 'other', but this is one of those things I think sounds unwieldy, and which is the mark of a beginning worldmaker. Maybe use hours or simply say something like she doesn't know how long it is since she slept, then you can have the Master examine her face shrewdly, nod and say, "At least 24 hours I'd say"."

~ Isobelle Carmody

There's no need to be so obvious, world building is about subtlety, not ambushing your reader with a sledgehammer. Below is a more subtle example of world building that Isobelle complimented. Notice that it tells you a bit about the advances of the society, and implies the relationship between magic and technology in this world without being in your face:

Around the circumference of the room were multiple green spheres, composed of some sort of liquid with fanning ripples moving continuously along the surface. Each sphere was next to a shining silver desk with a person staring at a mirrored surface. Some were talking into a type of headset, made of a simple mesh of Lines like a screen before their eyes, and a ball on the end of a little stick that hung before their lips. Each desk had a smaller mirror under the larger one. In the larger mirror some of the operators were moving different pieces of information about the surface with precise, complicated hand movements, manipulating Lines of Power.

~ Priori

"Lovely visual images merging magic and technology – I really like that aspect of your story."

~ Isobelle Carmody

4: What's Good, What's Bad?

It's the dichotomy between these two that will cause conflict. Don't make the mistake of assuming the whole world is the same. A world is made up of a patch work of different cultures, heck even Star Trek is made up of different races with different cultures (even if Earth is supposed to be this one harmonious whole). What is considered good or bad in a different culture? How do these collide?

5: Create Characters Who Plausibly Fit into this New World

External environment has a way of changing how people

EMILY CRAVEN

react and think; the same thing goes for your imaginary world. In *Priori*, one group of people live in a city hidden beneath the ocean (Creana) and come to rescue my main character, Beverly, on the surface. One of my writers' group members pointed out that at no point during their stint on the surface did they marvel at the stars. Which got me to thinking about all of the other things which would be foreign to them that I never once addressed: beaches, direct rays from the sun, an ocean breeze, an extreme range of temperatures and animal and plant life. I can't have Beverly marvelling at their underwater world without having them do the same in return.

So that's the quick and dirty five. Now start building! Or rebuilding as the case may be.

Exercise

One of the basic ways to make sure you build world and a character's place in it is to imagine what in a new setting would fascinate a particular character. Hence the exercise below:

- Step 1: Pick two or three of the below character/scenery transitions to work with.

   ◦ A city boy coming to the country

   ◦ A country girl coming to the city

○ A person who lives underwater coming to the surface

○ A person who lives in a palace finding themselves in the slums

○ A landlubber who finds themselves in space

○ A middle class mother meeting her son's upper class mother in law for the first time.

• Step 2: How would the switches in scenery in Step 1 affect the character? What would they notice? What could get them into trouble? What could they mistakenly assume was dangerous? What could they mistakenly assume is *not* dangerous? Write down your assumptions to start getting you into the rhythm.

• Step 3: Now look at any major transitions in scenery for characters in your own work. Make a note of the things that they would find different (using the questions in step 2) and try to work some of that into your scenes.

The below Golden Moment is a combination of the first three notes in this chapter, I had to make sure I did my 'research', I wanted the medallions which the community used to do magick to be different to wands or other magical objects you come across in fantasy novels. The below begins to set up the rules for the magic in this world, not going into super fine detail and making it awkward, just providing enough to imply the rest. You'll also note that the information dump is broken up by action and description so it's not as dense for the reader.

Golden Moments

"Remember, a Medallion is not like a magickal object in the old stories from the Surface. These stories hint that the object taps into your magickal abilities. On the contrary, your Medallions are just focusing instruments that help you to see the Lines of Power near you clearly and use them easily."

From the folds of my apprentice jacket, I removed my Medallion, the smooth gems gleamed in an otherwise ordinary metal setting. It was amazing to think that something so small held the key to accessing a world full of magick. In bare seconds Lines appeared before my eyes, delicate strands each straight as an arrow, passing through all objects including the bodies of the surrounding students.

"The Lines of Power are all around you, they are the never ending source of all the worlds' magick; they are the building blocks of all life. As the objects created by Line magick slowly break down or are destroyed, the magick is returned to whence it came, completing the Circle of Magick. You pull and focus your ability along these Lines."

ORIGINAL FANTASY

~ Priori

Line

BEGINNINGS PART 2 - CAST A SPELL IN THE FIRST LINE

Beginnings are important. They are your fishing lure, your spider's web, your black hole from which there is no return until series end. It is what a new reader will judge you on, an editor will judge you on, an agent will judge you on. Frankly anyone who can read, and is looking at your book will judge you on it. No pressure. In genre I would break beginnings up into two areas, your first lines and the meddlesome backstory in your first chapters. I spoke previously about my prelude/prologue vendetta in the structural section, so in this chapter I'll focus on first lines.

First lines seem like they wouldn't be a problem, I mean you have to write at least 20,000 sentences when writing your novel. That is until you start to look at the first line of your favourite authors' books and realise how calculated they are, written to suck away your soul and hold it until that last page. I strive for my first sentences to be as dynamic as my favourite authors; some examples of first sentences from my favourite books are below:

Riding back to the old neighbourhood felt like I had come a lot further than a few suburbs, maybe back in time. I found myself thinking of his mother, the witch queen, wondering if she would tell me where he was.

~ Green Monkey Dreams: The Witch Seed, Isobelle Carmody

The drought that gripped Ros's family's farm broke the year he started hearing voices.

~ The Changeling, Sean Williams

The magical activities of Britain have always been highly organised. Anyone who doubts this should consider the Spanish Armada and the winds that so conveniently dissipated it – and perhaps further consider why even the most sceptical of historians accepts this convenient hurricane so calmly, as a perfectly natural occurrence.

~ A Sudden Wild Magic, Diana Wynne Jones

All of them start at a point of intrigue or in the middle of some turning point or important event. You will notice none of them start in a backstory or a prelude. My first sentence for my fantasy manuscript, *Priori*, is by no means perfect and has gone through many incarnations, all of them changed for one reason or another:

It's so clear in my mind. A story unlike any other, a story my dear brother told me long ago. I was only a child.

~ Priori – 2005

Gah! Starts off with a prelude and the main character's voice is stilted and snobbish. Move on.

Cautiously we set out, quickly disappearing into the forest at the back of the property. Making as little noise as possible we made our way to the side gate.

~ Priori – March 2010

Complete floating background. The description is too vague and the image of the surrounds does not firmly ground you in the story. There are also a lot of adverbs (-ly words). Adverbs should be used as little as possible in good writing, not to say you can't keep one or two – I'm more than guilty of missing them during my editing passes. This is because adjectives *tell* people rather than *show* them.

Showing your reader the 'caution' in that character's movement makes for a more dynamic description, also the more your reader makes the emotional leap for themselves, the more they invest in your story.

There were two options. I was either going to get out of this alive and be running for my life for weeks or I'd be dead before I left the county.

~ Priori – June 2010

Firstly, the second line is awkward, the words trip over each other to get a simple idea across. I was trying to fit too much in, noting the time span needed to get to safety etc. Secondly, the reader does not know who 'I' is nor what county they are talking about. They don't care or know about the character so this beginning isn't good at evoking emotion or drawing the reader in.

Finally fate had thrust me forward. I had to run for my life or I'd be dead before I left the county.

~ Priori – March 2011

The first sentence is good; it says something momentous is happening. Also, I know as a reader of fantasy novels I always wish something fantastic would happen in my life and thrust me forward. It is my hope this first sentence will tap into that reader desire and use it to pull them in. The second sentence, though simplified from the above, again has the same problem of this unknown 'I' and county. Better to have some sort of description to build tension and ground the reader in the scene.

Finally fate had thrust me forward. Too loud, my breath rattled in the frigid air.

~ Priori – May 2012

This is where my first lines are at now. The second sentence tells you there is a need for silence and caution and tells you something about the surrounds. Originally the second sentence said cold air; finding this too plain I tried chilled before I settled on frigid. There is still the unknown 'I', however this has been solved by mentioning the name of the character in the next paragraph.

Before test readers went through the manuscript the first mention of the character's name, Beverly, was on page 8. This resulted in readers believing the main character was in fact a boy and getting a huge shock when this turned out not to be so. The last thing I want is for readers to be jerked out of the story by an unintentional gender change.

Crafting of first lines does not stop there; they must be carefully done for each chapter. Each new chapter must draw the reader in so they are constantly turning the page, and each chapter ending must leave the reader hanging in some way to make them want to keep reading. An example of the changes suggested by Isobelle to the start of my second chapter are below:

The brilliant blue sky wheeled above and the horse's hooves continued to trample past. I knew I had knocked out a tooth that day. What I hadn't known was it would be the catalyst that released my power and all the pain the Priori brought with it.

~ Priori – Draft

I was ten when I knocked out a tooth; I had thought it funny, falling off the horse face first into the mud. The brilliant blue sky had wheeled above and the horse's hooves continued to trample past.

~ Priori – Rewrite

The original was confusing for we did not know if the riding was happening in the past or the future, it is best to clarify changes in time to avoid confusing the reader. Isobelle suggested it was better to note the age of the character and to jump straight into reliving the scene. It is a minor change but one that brought clarity to the story.

It is these little tweaks that need to be made in the 'final' editing stages (if one can ever consider their editing truly finished).

So my humble recommendation is to take note of your first lines, and the first lines of every novel you ever read. Because the writers who make it far (or like me, hope to make it far) pay attention to the detailed mechanics as well as the whole story.

Exercise

So you've decided you need to brush up on your first lines. They're resembling a text book on accounting more than a thrilling adventure. That's fine, that's fixable. The solution to your first line troubles are below, young apprentice...

Part 1

- Step 1: Grab your favourite books off the shelf or key them up on your ereader (limit yourself to ten... yes I know it's hard... well frankly this whole writing business is hard, so if you can't pick ten books... fine, if you want to do extra work, I'll let you pick 15) and then record the first two lines of each novel.

- Step 2: Now categorise them: Do they deal with action? Scenery? Or character/dialogue?

- Step 3: Out of all the lines you recorded, which ones appeal to you most, and what category are they? This is probably your dominant style of first line; file this information away in the neurons for later reference.

- Step 4: Take your favourite of the ten books (flip a coin if you have to, or draw names out of a hat if you've fallen down a well of indecision) and write down the first two lines of every chapter. Also note which of the three categories they fall under

- Step 5: Which of the three styles; action, scene, or character/dialogue, is the most dominant? What is it about those lines that are intriguing? *This sense of intrigue* is what you are trying to emulate in your own writing. Once you understand what you respond to (and hence what your potential audience responds to) you have a better understanding of how to strategically structure your first words.

Part 2

Time for experimentation. Now that you know what type of sentences pique your interest, try writing some of your own!

- Step 1: Rewrite the first sentence of your novel

or short story in your dominant style (e.g. action).

- Step 2: Now rewrite it so you're grounding the reader in the scene, then by drawing them in via dialogue or character musing etc.

- Step 3: If you have written a novel, do this for the start of every chapter of your story and pick the most vivid of the three as your new first sentence for that chapter.

Examples

Perhaps now is a good point to give you some examples of first lines from several short stories I have written. Note my dominant style is most definitely action, followed in some cases by second sentences grounding the reader in the scenery. For the short story, *Teddy Bears' Picnic*, which was published in *Tincture Journal* in November 2014, I had two versions of the first line, but decided the 'action' first line gave away too much information so swapped if for the 'scenery' first line.

Teddy Bears do not exist in Camdale anymore; not since the picnic. They were piled high and consumed by fire. Their demise was accompanied by a strangled cheer akin to a war cry, amplified by the huts that surrounded the square.

~ Teddy Bears' Picnic – Action

In the beginning, Browning Forest was a nothing wood. It extended leagues to the east, pines tall, close-spaced and uninteresting.

~ Teddy Bears' Picnic – Scenery

Other opening sentences from my short stories include...

No one had knocked on that door for years. The unfamiliar thumping startled the gardener to wakefulness.

~ The Gardener

'No look! No touch!' The picture of the garden was easy to miss for it blended in harmoniously with the shadows. It was old and faded, but when caught by the eyes it was strangely compelling.

~ The Ethereals

I call my method Road Kill, though it's trickier than it sounds. First, you have to get them on the open road, then, figure out how to get them to cross the highway.

~ 300 Miles to Brisbane

I glared at Ariki Tekuma, the chieftain of Tavake village.
His eyes twitched from me back to the bundle of Mata
pendants I'd thrust into his hands.

~ A Cook's Statue

It has been hours; time ticking away too quickly to the
deadline. Why would The Alchemist, a person with his skills,
dwell in this substandard level of society with its decaying stench?
They'd been using manufactured scents to mask reality since my
father's day, but these were not the quality smells available in the
markets.

~ The Alchemist

The Golden Moment below is the first line of Chapter 10, about half way through the *Priori* story. It is one of the very few times in the book where I begin with description. This is because the rest of the chapter is informational, a chapter where Beverly is learning about the magic systems and how to control her own magick, something she sees as being fraught with danger. In her experience, the Priori has only ever 'blown stuff up', so to speak...

Golden Moments

Within the first week, I found out that everything I took for granted to be normal, turned out to involve copious amounts of magick or could be altered by magick to improve its usefulness. It was astonishing, the amount of science one could mix with magick to create objects that could perform amazing feats beyond that of everyday mechanical jobs. Today was to be my first official attempt at manipulating the Lines of Power.

~ Priori

SAY IT SIMPLY - SEVEN WAYS TO AVOID OVERWRITING

IF THE BEGINNING GETS UNDER YOUR SKIN
THEN SEEK PARAGRAPH TWO.

Here I sit in a padded seat, soft and squishy against my sharp, angular pelvic bones, in an airtight cabin transporting myself and those around me in an aerial manner to the grouping of buildings known as Melbourne. The salty tang of the flattened potato, crisped via heat transference, triggers my cerebellum's craving for liquid sustenance to quench the parched state of my throat and mouth.

In other words, I'm sitting in an aeroplane on my way to Melbourne and have just taken a large gulp of water because the Pringles were too salty. Ok, I may have gone a bit overboard in my demonstration, but overwriting is rife within genre fiction and particularly fantasy/sci-fi. Simple equals more. More clarity, greater pace, and an all-around smoother ride for your reader. You don't care whether or not my seat is comfortable, and if you did, the fact that I used the word 'comfortable' rather than the entire first line has made your reading a little more understandable. Just because you're able to expand a description doesn't mean it's clever to do so; like inflating an aeroplane life vest, you can do it, but after you meet the police at the gate it no longer seems wise.

Water droplets from the recent storm were sprinkled as far as the eye could see, reflecting the sunlight's colours on Charlie's face.

~ Priori – Draft

"With fantasy, which is epic and dramatic by its very nature, I think it is always better to strive for directness and simplicity, particularly in word choice. Droplet is the same as drop, but fancier, and unnecessary."

~ Isobelle Carmody

Vorx's yellow light reflected from a scatter of raindrops onto Charlie's face.

~ Priori – Rewrite

As Isobelle said, the original was just a fancy way of

saying light reflected from the water onto Charlie's face. Also, if there were raindrops on the ground, it is very obvious it rained recently. The second iteration was shorter, concise and picking a colour gave the scene a mood.

Most overwriting (or 'the brown bits' as I like to call them) is a result of not having thought clearly about what you want to say and how to say it. In some cases, it comes from the belief that a wordy description will help to show characterisation when in fact it adds nothing and holds the story back rather than moving it forward.

I found during my writing mentorship that there are seven ways in which I can tighten my prose to avoid overwriting and create vivid images in the reader's mind rather than vague impressions. Let's examine how NOT to confuse your reader, and just tell the damn story!

1: Too Much Explanation/Overwriting

One of the best ways to remove the floweriness is to try cutting the number of words in a sentence. Look for the shortest way to say it and only then, if it's looking a little bare without its summer leaves, add a single flourish or unusual word into the mix. In this way the ornate word is there when it will really say something. Like any emerging writer I have an entire goody bag of overwritten sentences, which I (stupidly?) have provided below to help you recognise this in your own writing:

A sudden shiver shook me violently.

~ Priori – Draft

I shuddered.

~ Priori – Rewrite

Shiver and shook are the same thing. Why use the word violently when you can merge all three into one, relevant word – shuddered?

I struggled to suppress the sudden moistness inhibiting my vision.

~ Priori – Draft

To my chagrin I felt tears pricking my eyes.

~ Priori – Rewrite

I know, when I read 'sudden moistness' in my re-read I groaned out loud too. This is where trying to be 'different' back-fired. On the plus side, now we know even more about Beverly's personality because of the addition of 'chagrin' in relation to her tears.

She looked genuinely flattered at the respectful tone I had unconsciously adopted.

~ Priori – Draft

She looked pleased.

~ Priori – Rewrite

The audience doesn't need me to point out the respect in the previous dialogue if I have written it correctly!

"I was listening, sir," I answered then cursed my impulse to say such a thing. Now I would have to prove my attendance to his lesson before we could move on. If I did not the lesson would simply end until I had learnt it on my own and proved I had memorised it in full.

~ Priori – Draft

"I was listening, sir," I answered without thought.

~ Priori – Rewrite

Why would the reader need me to explain what I am going to make the other character do in the next couple of paragraphs (namely, halt his teaching until she could prove it)? This overly detailed description I had originally put in to 'add tension'. However, I was trying to add tension from nothing and the little monologue did nothing to move the story forward.

The initially light weighted drape of my brother's arm gradually became a heavy handed clutch as we continued to move forward.

~ Priori – Draft

Gradually, Charlie's lightweight touch on my shoulder became a painful clutch, fingers digging into flesh.

~ Priori – Rewrite

The original wording was clumsy, what does a heavy-handed clutch even mean? By taking my time to choose the right words, and what I wanted to convey in that action (that Charlie was upset about something), I got a cleaner sentence.

The portal that had been there only seconds ago was no more, as though it had never been.

~ Priori – Draft

The portal that had been there only seconds ago had vanished.

~ Priori – Rewrite

Should I insult your intelligence by explaining why I changed that?

2: Filler Phrases

We all have those little filler words we use in conversation: 'just', 'only', 'seemed', 'that', 'if you know what I mean' etc. These are fine in every day conversation but are place holders in prose, piles of junk that plague all writers. In addition to filler words, if you have one of these filler phrases like the one in the below example, search and destroy in your manuscript!

I was not under any circumstance going to let myself get caught on my first invisible outing.

~ Priori – Draft

I was not going to let myself get caught on my first invisible outing.

3: Unnecessary Time Delineation

Like those filler phrases, every writer will also find some sort of unnecessary delineation of time. The passing of time in a well written novel will always be shown through action rather than telling the audience that time passes, as in the example below.

For several minutes the only sound in the room was the shuffling of papers from the direction of Madam Cinder's desk in the back corner of the room.

~ Priori – Draft

The only sound in the room was the shuffling of papers from the direction of Madam Cinder's desk.

~ Priori – Rewrite

4: If You've Implied it, Don't State it

One thing that annoys the pants off me is when a writer does a wonderful job of implying, but then unconsciously assumes 'reader don't read good' and then tells me what they did subtly. Take Twilight for example. There are dozens of instances where a character will 'shout loudly', or 'whisper quietly'. A shout will be loud, and a whisper quiet, the volume is embedded in the word's meaning, there is no need to include the dictionary. And sometimes this implication/explanation pair can be caused by stating two actions when a single action is a sufficient substitute for both.

I must be going crazy, talking to voices inside my head, he thought. Ones that don't even exist.

~ Priori – Draft

I must be going crazy, screaming at a voice inside my head, he thought.

~ Priori – Rewrite

Unless we have been told otherwise, the reader will assume a voice that talks inside your head doesn't exist, this is an unnecessary sentence (unless your audience is comprised of schizophrenics).

The pacing stopped momentarily as he collapsed onto a wooden stool.

~ Priori – Draft

He collapsed onto a wooden stool.

~ Priori – Rewrite

If he collapses onto a stool, we do not need to be told that he has stopped pacing momentarily; he would have to, to be able to sit!

5: Word Order

Sometimes you have all the right words, but suddenly suffer from creative dyslexia. All that's required is a little rearranging to get your meaning across...

...for conducting dangerous experiments and inadvertently killing thirty people against the expressed wishes of his superior...

~ Priori – Draft

...for conducting dangerous experiments against the expressed wishes of his superior, and inadvertently killing thirty people...

~ Priori – Rewrite

The change needed to occur otherwise it sounded as

if the superior was forbidding him to kill thirty people, rather than the superior forbidding he do dangerous experiments.

6: Too Many Adjectives

We all love our descriptors (I am especially guilty of this). I was of the opinion when I started writing that the more adjectives I strung together, the better the picture I would paint. Yes, I was a little naive. Because what I was showing was I hadn't taken the time to find the *right* word and used this adjective list to make up for my lack of clarity. On your next read through of your writing, keep an eye out for your own lists of adjectives. Remember, one good adjective is best, and sometimes none is better still.

As the glow dimmed so did the sharp, raw pain of what must have been a spectacular bruise.

~ Priori – Draft

As the glow dimmed so did the raw pain of what must have been a spectacular bruise.

~ Priori – Rewrite

Raw is a stronger, more evocative word.

7: Be Precise

Choosing the right words is a royal pain in the bum. Because more often than not, you find your word bag broken. If you could just reach in and pluck out that word on the edge of your thoughts you would be sweet. Most of the time, I shove something in there so I can get on with the writing. However, in the rewrites I have to drag out my thesaurus and beat my mind into submission as in the example below. In my next chapter, I will be going into more detail about the importance of choosing the right words in your editing.

My hand slipped into the warm puddle, covering my forearms in water and thick russet red mud.

~ Priori – Draft

My hand slipped into the warm puddle, splashing my forearms with water and thick russet mud.

~ Priori – Rewrite

In this instance only her hand has moved into the puddle, therefore her forearms could not be completely 'covered in' water, only 'splashed with' water. At the end of the sentence you also saw a list of adjectives, I needed to choose one, red *or* russet, rather than having both.

This section may seem picky, but these seven writing boo-boos are responsible for most reader confusion. And you don't want them to be confused; you want them to consume your novel like a tasty dessert.

Exercise

In this exercise let's start simplifying your work.

- Step 1: Pick a scene from your work in progress that needs a bit of cleaning up (or has gotten a lot of comments from your writers group!).

- Step 2: Do seven individual editing passes focusing on one of the points below in each pass of the scene.

  ○ Remove over-explaining – reduce to a few simple words.

  ○ Remove filler words and phrases like: 'just', 'only', 'seemed', 'that', 'if you know what I mean' etc.

  ○ Remove unnecessary time delineations.

- If you've implied it, don't state it.
- Change word order to make things clearer.
- Remove your adjectives
- Be precise in your word choice/imaginings.

The Golden Moment for this chapter seems simple enough, but it took five to six passes of editing, of rearranging words, removing fill phrases and picking the right descriptors until I had a smooth, simple set of sentences for this rather complex visual.

Golden Moments

The interrogation ended as suddenly as it had started. She pinched a Line of Power from seemingly nowhere and drew out a flat shining rectangle that dimmed into a sheaf of papers which she handed to me.

~ Priori

EMOTING – OVERWRITING ROUND 2

I'm not alone in thinking 80s action movies are the bomb. Terminator, Speed, Predator – if it has a man with an accent, some guns (mechanical or biological) and an Arnie Abs close up – I know I'll be in for fun-times. Action keeps up the pace, it's what we forgive bad special effects for, and balances all the necessary tension building and WTF moments at the start. Actor getting it on with a llama? Forgiven with a shirtless scene. Pensive looks into the distance? Forgotten at the first sky dive from a space ship in a g-string while using an oversized t-shirt as a parachute.

We don't need the actor telling us they are scared, or sad, or happy or f-ed both ways to Tuesday. Their face says it, their language says it, their tone says it, the dramatic German-techno-rave-soundtrack-with-Bowie-samples says it.

As a writer I used to think that I had to pack all the dorky awesomeness of an 80s movie into my book. I had to show people exactly how my character was feeling because how would they know unless I told them? They couldn't see it, I had to describe it all, right? Wrong. While the thought seemed logical, it had the habit of giving readers in good health a sudden spike in blood pressure. If you don't understand why, let's go back to the 80's action movie example.

Say the bad guy has cornered the good guy, and explosions are going off like a five year old at a light switch. Now, imagine between the 'Bam!' and 'Pow!' of a good right hook, the action pauses for five seconds to allow the character to articulate exactly how they were feeling when the baddie called their mother a spotted hyena from Mercury with a bad nose job. Then several 'Bangs!' and 'Kablams!' later the action pauses again for the main character to articulate their surprise at being jumped from behind by a minion with a pool cue. And then this continues for the rest of the scene.

Even the most mild-mannered viewer is going to say, "Listen, you spent the whole movie showing me his bloody personality, I understand Your-Mamma jokes press his buttons. Do YOU understand that you're pissing me off? Perhaps your ideal audience has an IQ in the negatives. I'm going to watch Star Wars now to calm the heck down."

It doesn't work, on screen or paper.

When you reach a scene a reader has been waiting for, whether it be action or the unveiling of some long awaited information, cutting down on emotional words will make your scene more powerful, not less. Because you are allowing the reader to feel the emotion themselves, you're not assuming they're a few peanuts short of an elephant snack. Over emoting you character is very easy to do, and hard to convince yourself to cut, but there are several key reasons why you should be ruthless with your emotional telling:

1: It's Repetitive

Do it too often and the reaction becomes nothing new, and when you really need that impact, you fall into cliché. In my initial version of *Priori*, this became a problem in the final half of the manuscript:

> *From there the fear began to mount, creeping in at first but quickly building up momentum. I screamed, but instead of the dream dissolving, it continued with terrifying clarity...*
> *What did such a dream mean? That I would kill Charlie?*

~ Priori – Draft

"Well, the 'you'll kill him' is obvious. I think this whole paragraph, particularly the first sentence, is over emoting- you do this often enough that you need to watch it in yourself. You have a

sentence, in which your character reacts dramatically to something, and we are given a lot of physical detail, but none of it feels particularly fresh or surprising so more often than not, I would cut it. At the least the reader feels irritated and patronised, at the worst it makes your character look like they are over acting. If the reaction is something we could extrapolate from an event then don't bother telling us what the character feels, unless you are sure it is going to surprise the reader in some way, or unless the description of the fear is unusual or unusually beautiful. Otherwise it makes the writing feel overly attenuated."

~ Isobelle Carmody

There stood Charlie, shocked and bewildered, his hand reaching forward as if he could ward off the approaching magick with his will alone. The ball hit him square in the chest, entering his body like an arrowhead. He was consumed by white flames from the inside out, fully enveloped in a matter of seconds. "CHARLIE!!!!!" I screamed as the flames consumed him, spreading to the staircase and all he was near. I dropped to my knees. The dream dissolved, leaving me to battle with sorrow in the darkness.

~ Priori – Rewrite

2: Your Readers are Generally Smarter than You

By taking over an action scene with all this emoting, you are usurping the reader's ability (nay, their pleasure) to react to the scene for themselves. You're assuming they can't infer things, and frankly, you're pissing them off. In the below example from the initial *Priori* manuscript, Isobelle tells me to have faith in my ability to tell a story without bashing my readers over the head with a therapist (*and how does that make you feel?*).

Another contributing factor was my nervousness at attending my first Circle of Magick. My thoughts turned to how they would react, a group of experienced Enchanters, to a teenager who knew next to nothing and was the reason for such a grave meeting. At the least they would be disgruntled. At the most they would gaze at me in reverence even though I had landed them in this predicament. That would be one reaction I could not stand.

~ Priori – Draft

"Again seems muddled. What is she actually feeling? At the moment it feels as if you are trying to inject emotion artificially by having her do a lot of emoting, when in fact this is such a dramatic series of events you ought to be letting them happen and allowing the reader to react rather than usurping this. Trust yourself as a writer, trust that the events you have set up – your story – is good enough to make them respond with feelings rather than trying to ensure it. The ability to trust your readers to be at least as smart as you are is the mark of a fine writer. I understand that she might feel muddled and anxious, but she ought also to

begin to see it is her role. Let us see her thoughts, just cut down on having her emote. This is another form of overwriting."

~ Isobelle Carmody

It took me three tries before I could mount with my fluid legs. The trip through the fabric between worlds was more draining than I had first assumed. Or perhaps it was my trepidation at attending my first Circle of Magick. Would they despise me for destroying their peace? I pushed the thought to one side. There was no point in dwelling on it, I would see soon enough.

~ Priori – Rewrite

*

Tears streamed down my face to fall into the relentless tide of the river.

~ Priori – Draft

"This is a tragic event, but one of the problems with writing out such events is that we have to be careful not to usurp the reader's response. When you edit this section try cutting all of her emotional reactions and simply let the action stand, then replace maybe one or two phrases or words that imply her state of mind, and which do so beautifully and originally, because obviously the reader knows how she must feel. So you must strive to say the

thing that had not been thought of, but which will seem true the second they read it."

~ Isobelle Carmody

My tears fell into the relentless tide of the river.

~ Priori – Rewrite

Yes, by all means let the readers see your character's thoughts, but cut down on the emoting. Your readers are probably smarter than you and deserve your respect. This is another form of overwriting and something to be avoided like an oompa-loompa oompa-band.

Exercise

It's time to pull out all of those emotional tags and see if your writing – the dialogue, the action, the descriptions etc. stand on their own.

- Step 1: Take your highest action or conflict scene and remove all emotive words from around your dialogue. Some examples of emotive words/actions include:

  ◦ Red hot anger,

- ○ Impotent rage,

- ○ Tears,

- ○ Fear

- ○ Terrify

- ○ Nervous, etc.

- **Step 2:** Make sure that when you remove those descriptors you have strong language/verbs in your dialogue to help convey the emotion of the moment.

- **Step 3:** Now get someone you trust to beta read the scene and ask them to note in the margins what they are feeling as they read through the scene. From there you can see if you have struck the right balance of conveying emotion while trusting your reader.

The Golden Moment below contained large amounts of emoting before I rewrote it for my mentorship with Isobelle. I left in a few choice emotional words to make the scene pop but removed half a dozen others. It was wonderful to see that the pared back section seemed to strike a chord.

Golden Moments

The girl gasped only to be silenced by a hand on her mouth as pale as her own.

"Three guesses what you're doing here," he said.

She pushed his hand away and glared at him. He looked almost identical to her, the same pale skin but with slight differences. His coal black hair was shorter and his features more masculine but it was clear they were, in every way, twins.

"Just who I was looking for," she replied.

He rolled his eyes. "I know your game, I heard it too you know. I'm not going and neither are you."

"I am going," she said fiercely, "You don't have to come."

~ Priori

CHOOSING THE RIGHT ERECTION – WAIT! I MEAN 'WORD'

"It is wise always to look at the words you use closely, because the standard of writing is lifted immensely by anyone prepared to take the time to search for exactly the right word. It sounds mad but I have sometimes spent a whole day just trying to describe something as faithfully and well as I can."

~ Isobelle Carmody

On first glance it seems a very involved bit of advice for the phrase '*My breath rattled*'. "Which is fine," Isobelle assured me in this instance, "However, it is used a LOT in writing and it's wise to always look at the words you use closely..." She is right of course.

A single word can change the tone of an entire paragraph, it can confuse a reader, create the wrong image, or prove that we don't know our dictionary meanings very well. This is the nuts and bolts of writing, this is how a reader knows you are a great writer rather than a good storyteller. This is how a book gets added to the favourites list to be reread rather than read and forgotten.

Sometimes, finding the right word sucks peanuts. But it's worth it. I always find examples are the best way to really drum a lesson into the head (particularly one that your ego would rather not learn) so below are a few of my 'less considered' writing moments of the past that I've learned from and used to grow my spidey-sense for the badly chosen word.

1: The Wrong Tone

One word in the wrong tone can throw off a whole page. You may have worked hard to build the tension, create danger and then you use that one word and suddenly your atmosphere and your characterisation come unravelled...

The distant sound of jiggling weapons...

~ Priori – Draft

"Jiggling seems wrong; you need a more threatening word for the sound weapons make when their bearers run with them."

~ Isobelle Carmody

The distant sound of rattling weapons...

~ Priori – Rewrite

Yep, I had created the Santa Claus version of war, correction made.

Charlie reached out stabilising me as I slipped sideways, my body unable to support itself, and shifted next to me so I could lean on him.

~ Priori – Draft

"Seems rather a formal lot of words for a brother steadying his distraught younger sister. This word choice is affecting characterisation – these words do not suggest the tenderness and concern of a good older brother for his younger sister. Try to make the words you choose echo what is being said in tone."

~ Isobelle Carmody

Unable to support myself, my body slipped sideways. Alarmed, Charlie rushed in to steady me. He drew me to his chest. I

*collapsed against him, grateful for his warm arms and their
tender support.*

~ Priori – Rewrite

Somehow he had become a robot brother, damn, probably happened because I only have sisters... well that's my excuse. Correction made.

*They kept the Empire on its toes and in most cases just barely kept
the Empire from randomly executing people.*

~ Priori – Draft

*"Again look at the tone of these words, this is a cosy colloquial
sort of phrase and seems oddly matched with this Empire."*

~ Isobelle Carmody

*They kept the Empire on edge, in some ways making them
crueller and swifter in their retribution.*

~ Priori – Rewrite

Damn clichés being the first words to come into my head, must remember to catch and destroy before they embed themselves in the page, correction made.

2: Reader Confusion & Unintended Images

Applying the wrong action to a person or animal or giving emotions/emotional description to an inanimate object can stop a reader in their tracks. This results in a moment where the reader says, "Hmm... that doesn't match." I now see it as a sign that I didn't have a clear picture in my head before I began writing.

We pulled our mounts to a furtive stop behind a thick hedge.

~ Priori – Draft

"Are they leading the horses or on them? Leading would make more sense given the need for stealth. I would cut 'furtive', it is implied and voicing it makes us wonder how mounts can be furtively pulled."

~ Isobelle Carmody

Instant image of a cartoon character tip-toeing while leading a horse wearing slippers. It seemed to make so much sense in my head, if only I'd transferred it correctly to the page. Right again Isobelle, correction made.

*Rusted and old, the shed embodied everything I hated about my
mother, the cold separation, the rotting interior.*

~ Priori – Draft

*"I am not sure the words 'cold separation' can be applied to a
hut, perhaps 'the cold shell', 'the hard carapace' or maybe simply
have her want to destroy something to vent her rage, and do it."*

~ Isobelle Carmody

*Rusted and old, the shed embodied everything I hated about my
mother, the cold shell, and empty heart.*

~ Priori – Rewrite

If the hut is embodying the things she hated then I
needed words that befitted a hut as well as a person, not
words that projected emotions onto an inanimate object.

*The warm, loving embrace of the light from the earth's two suns,
Kelt and Vorx, enfolded me.*

~ Priori – Draft

*"Be careful of using emotional terms like 'loving' for physical
phenomena, it can seem mawkish."*

~ Isobelle Carmody

Perhaps it comes from me believing my teddies loved me as a child. Correction made.

Little by little a crackly voice inched its way slowly through my ears.

~ Priori – Draft

"This is awkward, 'crackly' is vague and sound does not 'inch' and 'into' would be better than 'through'."

~ Isobelle Carmody

Little by little a voice secreted its way into my ears and registered in my brain.

~ Priori – Draft

Unless the character had a tunnel from one ear to the other, Isobelle was completely right. Correction made.

Muttered curses exploded from one voice mere inches from the cave entrance...

~ Priori – Draft

"A voice does not explode. A curse might explode from

someone, or muttered curses might explode mere inches from the cave."

~ Isobelle Carmody

3: Using Words that are Unnatural in Normal Conversation

"You see Bev..."

~ Priori – Draft

"To use the name of someone close over and over is unnatural – if you think about it, we almost don't use the names of people we know to their faces, and only use the name to call them or to refer to them."

~ Isobelle Carmody

If I kept using my partner's name every time I spoke to him I'm pretty sure he'd either think I was angry with him or sit me down with a cold compress and a gag until the phase passed. Correction made.

4: Words Where We Forgot the Meanings (Or Alternate

Meanings)

In the quest for an unusual word to spice up the prose we sometimes pick words that don't cut the mustard.

Within seconds of it leaving my mouth I saw her form swarm up through the water dragon and out of one of its claws.

~ Priori – Draft

"Swarm suggests the movement of more than one, of many in fact. Perhaps use 'rise'."

~ Isobelle Carmody

Finally, to end I'd like to give you an example where the literal meaning of a word has quite the alternate meaning in the modern vocabulary. Hopefully it gives you a big smile to carry with you for the rest of the day...

"That is Oceana Academy," said Satinay excitedly, pointing towards the majestic erection before us.

~ Priori – Draft

"Hmmm, edifice/construct/demesne might be better..."

~ Isobelle Carmody

Oh dear, sorry Isobelle...

Exercise

Choosing the right word can be tricky, but worthwhile for the strong imagery it provides readers. This exercise will provide you a step-by-step plan to choosing that perfect word.

- **Step 1:** Pick a scene from your work in progress, maybe one that has been unwieldy, or one that is particularly long and may need a pickup in pace.

- **Step 2:** Do four individual editing passes, it might be a good idea to read the text out loud as you do these passes. Reading out loud stops you from skipping sentences you've read many times. In each pass concentrate on one of the points listed below:

  - Change words that evoke the wrong tone.

  - Make sure the right action/ description is applied to a person/ animal to avoid reader confusion.

- ° Remove unnatural words from dialogue.
- ° Watch out for words with alternate meanings.

In the Golden Moment below you will note the word choice is very simple, and specific and as a result provides a strong visual for the scene.

Golden Moments

He gripped both halves then pulled them further apart creating a gaping hole in reality. The hole was a dense black but at certain moments you could see tiny specks of raining light in a kaleidoscope of colours.

~ Priori

PACING – AVOID INTERRUPTING A READER'S FLOW

───────────

Pacing a story isn't as easy as it sounds and most writers don't realise they're self-sabotaging their work. Why? I sit here at my desk bleary eyed, my body crying out for some sort of warmth to justify leaving my bed this morning. Stephen King's On Writing sits to the right of me, as does a notebook and a box of tissues. The whirl of the air conditioner is depressing, why is it always work days where I'm so tired my face feels like a brick wall? Crap, I've been staring into space for ages now, what was I doing? Oh right, purposely interrupting your need to know exactly how I think you're self-sabotaging your work.

Sure that atmospheric description – sharing a little story that helps you connect with me, and with the work – is

───────
153

a good way of building character and world-building, but was that really the best place? No. Truth be told, you probably didn't care about that little piece of atmosphere, what you really wanted was to know how you were unknowingly sabotaging your work, bugger the description! By putting it there I was grabbing your coattails and pulling you to a stop, interrupting your expectation for the piece and the flow. The thing is, most of us do this naturally, in conversation we regularly wander off on tangents, but in real life we have tone, pitch, facial expressions, and large Italian hand movements to carry us through the wanderings and pick up again on the other side. In a book, your brain stops and re-reads if it feels it's missed something, breaking you out of 'the zone'.

When you talk to another person and go off on a tangent, their brain can't stop you in the middle of what you're saying (that would be rude!) so they must follow you or be left behind, hence why verbal stories can keep 'the flow'. However, if they have the option of stopping to consider, rather than diving into the tangent with you, they will. We write like we think and we think like we speak – it's natural. But our readers don't think the same as we do and *that* is the root of many a pacing problem. The trick is to know when description and introspection matter, because each has its place and that isn't during the middle of the reader's 'aha' moment.

You need to moderate pace to keep things interesting. This means a good mix between action, introspection and description. Large chunks of introspection and description can cause the pace to drag like a zombie leg. On the other end of the scale, if you have too many helicopter chases in a thriller the reader starts to skim over the narrative and detaches from the characters and their plight. By adding in a little bit of introspection into the action to explore personal stakes this will allow you to change things up a little.

It only takes a couple of misplaced lines, or even misplaced words to pull a reader out of the zone, whether it's unnecessary words, an observation at the wrong time, continuous noting about time passing or the character breaking into a retelling from another (future) time. Below are some examples of the interruptions to pacing Isobelle picked up in my draft of *Priori*. The underline indicates where the main problem lies:

1: Jumping in With Your Future Voice When Retelling a Past Event

"Ten years ago, before you were born, the Ruhle didn't reign over the world, they had only just promoted a new leader," Charlie began in a whisper.

"You lie," I choked.

He squeezed my hands, encouraged that I was listening.

"Remember I'm telling the truth," he said with a small smile.

Even then I can recall treating Charlie's tale as just a story with good and evil forces battling somewhere far removed from my reality. His shaking hands and darting eyes told me differently, but I chose not to see.

~ Priori – Draft

"This paragraph breaks the flow of the exciting events by breaking in from another time with an observation – I'd cut this. Maybe instead of calling her brother a liar, she can simply listen to a story we want to hear. She can call him a liar later, when we understand what it means."

~ Isobelle Carmody

*

Charlie told me later that it was a very strange sight to see us suddenly whisked vertically through the hole. Rooms flashed by as I was propelled upward. Mere seconds later I staggered heavily into Elitree in a foreign hall, with the silver star and circle under my feet and another hole above my head. The whole experience was unnervingly nauseating.

~ Priori – Draft

"Much more dramatic to stick with the girl's POV as she is drawn upward. Describe how it feels to her and what she sees, then run on, rather than shifting suddenly and inexplicably into a

single flashback on this moment. If you want, have him say it
later."

~ Isobelle Carmody

2: Unnecessary Words – Stating the Obvious

This point and the next has been mentioned previously in this guide, however I wanted reiterate them here as they have a sever effect on a novel's pacing.

Elitree, <u>seemingly oblivious to my discomfort</u>, started
introductions.

~ Priori – Draft

"Overwriting – focus on what is happening now, rather than
Beverly's minute reactions and emotions, especially since most of
them are pretty obvious responses to the situation, so a reader will
already fill that in."

~ Isobelle Carmody

3: Unnecessary Delineation of Time

"Wonderful,' I thought, <u>as the ground whorled closer</u>, 'I've fallen twice in one week.' <u>For a second</u>, the ground rushing closer with <u>each passing second</u>, I panicked.

~ Priori – Draft

"Too many unnecessary bulletins about time passing and words describing her movement. Get on with it – she is falling!"

~ Isobelle Carmody

4: Including Description/Observations at the Wrong Time

Never had I seen him so vexed before. His stern stance seem to enlarge him <u>as though he gathered power as though he were a bee keeper calling a swarm of angry bees to arms</u>.

~ Priori – Draft

"This is actually nice but it is too much here – typical overwriting and it really gets in the way in this moment when we are much more interested in what they are saying than how they look."

~ Isobelle Carmody

Freezing in mid-sentence <u>the slim lady</u> stared blankly ahead.

~ Priori – Draft

"Think of your character – would she really notice a woman is slim in the middle of this interaction? It is an unnecessary description. I quite like the idea that a feature of your character is her tendency to notice a lot, but maybe even mention that and perhaps have her frustrated by it."

~ Isobelle Carmody

Really, when I look back at this last one, the time to talk about this lady being slim is when she then turns from a thin woman in to a man with a moustache (no joke, it actually happens...).

5: Other Pacing Problems

While all of the above are specific pacing problems Isobelle caught within Priori, there are other ways you can fix pacing in a scene. If pace is dragging it is generally because:

- You have too much introspection and description. So consider cutting it, Samurai style, with economic swipes of your red pen sword.

- Your characters are behaving passively, they are waiting for things to happen to them or only reacting to events rather than being the instigator. By making them more active in their journey, you immediately make them a more interesting character as they are effecting change, even if it's only in a small manner.

- You have a string of really long sentences together. Writing shorter sentences immediately picks up the pace. In fact, action adventure writers like Matthew Reilly are famous for making sentences so short they rarely need commas.

- You have too much back story or there is an info dump hiding in the scene. The previous chapter about sprinkling your backstory should help you remedy this.

- You haven't spent enough time on the right thing. For example, you spend three paragraphs buying a sandwich and then only two sentences on getting mugged in the alley by a clown. Identify what part of the scene is the most important, or creates the most tension or mystery, and use that as your focal point.

While none of these examples seem overly dramatic, when you have many of them scattered throughout your manuscript it really affects the overall enjoyment for a reader, and can be the difference between a 3 star and a 5 star review.

Exercise

Wondering how to discover these road blocks in your own writing? Try this simple exercise below:

Part 1

- Step 1: Take a chapter from your manuscript and circle every instance where you describe time or state the obvious (you may find the number builds up quickly).

- Step 2: Remove these references from the chapter and see how it hangs together without them.

- Step 3: Hand your chapter to a beta reader and ask them to go through the chapter with you, then drill down on the places where you've removed things and make sure the message/ image still came across without further explanation.

Part 2

- Step 1: Pick one or two chapters and dot point the major parts in your scene. Basically you are reverse engineering an outline of the chapter.

- Step 2: Next to each point mark whether it is action (they are doing things or discussing things), introspection (they are thinking, reflecting, or remembering) or description (landscape, what people look like, how a plan is going to happen, some part of the backstory).

- Step 3: If you have paced the chapter well you should have an even spread of action, introspection and description across the chapter, though you may find that some chapters are led by a particular type (some chapters are more action driven, others more introspection driven). It's fine to have a leading type of pace, but you must make sure that the other two are evenly spread throughout the scene.

- Step 4: If you don't have an even spread, attempt to rearrange or remove the information such that you get a better pacing mix.

The Golden Moment in this chapter could have been slowed considerably by over explaining why they needed to make that sudden dash for cover. However the character didn't have to be clued in immediately. By waiting until a few sentences later, everything was explained, and didn't interrupt the action that came before.

Golden Moments

"Hurry. No time for explanations!" She pulled me sharply into a nearby shop as I craned my head over my shoulder to look at the billowing clouds. No sooner had we slipped inside when sheets of rain pelted from the sky forming an impenetrable waterfall. A few unlucky souls clung to each other as they struggled blindly through the deluge to their closest shelter.

"Flash storm," Fidleton gasped, flicking a few stray raindrops from her head. "They have them so things don't dry out. Unfortunately they don't give you any warning! It doesn't matter, we had to come here anyway." Fidleton glanced around to see if anybody was in the semi-dark room.

~ Priori

ATMOSPHERE THROUGH DESCRIPTION

___

When I first started writing I was unaware that the way you describe things affects the atmosphere of the scene. Not to say I was trying to put a sappy love scene in the middle of a bloody battlefield; I had read *some* books before I attempted my own! Of course, on an unconscious level I knew there was a difference between someone taking an arm and leading a person away, and someone grabbing an arm and jerking the person to one side. They are in essence the same movement or sequence of events but the words used in each convey very different images and moods. Creating a strong atmosphere is essential to a reader getting immersed in your words, so, I'd like to have a look at how you can use description to create atmosphere.

All writers fall into the trap at some point of telling

readers about the atmosphere rather than showing it. However, showing is always preferable as it plays on the reader's imagination and allows them to feel they are there with the character. See the effect showing rather than telling made to this scene from *Priori*:

I shivered. The place was so eerie, so magickal.

~ Priori – Draft

I shivered. The staircase had its own breeze, softly dancing around the tunnel, blowing our hair across our faces. It reminded me at once of the final line in the riddle, 'be swift as the breeze'. This seemed to be the final confirmation that we were in the right place. The voice of the wind chattered to us like an overexcited child, snatches of stolen conversation blown past too quick to make out. It always flowed forwards as though it were our guide.

~ Priori – Rewrite

The above tells us what is so magical (or magickal as I use in the novel) about the scene by drawing our attention to specifics. In the same way you can imply a situation or atmosphere as opposed to telling the reader outright. For example, instead of describing that the enemy is close, or a certain distance away, describe how clearly you can see their features. This implies your closeness, and makes the enemy more real:

Five Ruhle soldiers passed through our large iron gate a mere 600 feet away.

~ Priori – Draft

Five Ruhle soldiers were passing through our large iron gate. Their weapons clattered against brass plates sewn to leather, the ominous sound seeping through the trees. The final soldier passed so close I could see his pock-marked face, patchy hair growth and thuggish shoulders. He had an inking on his muscled upper arm; straight, black lines crossed off in batches of five. Thirteen lines in all. Marking what? Their skirmishes? Kills?

~ Priori – Rewrite

As you can see the description now calls on sound as well as visuals to describe the closeness as well as the dangerous quality of the soldiers.

You can also use description of a character to tell a reader about the surrounds, such as the quality of the light and hence the time of day. Or how a particular character views the person they are describing such as this passage below:

With barely an effort he mounted, stilling the beast in an instant with his gentle touch. My brother looked part of the horse; his short chestnut hair blazed in the last rays of daylight, matching the horse's hide. A tall young man when standing, his broad shoulders mirrored the strength of the beast's hindquarters. The dwindling light tinted his high cheek bones, the soft freckles and the piercing blue eyes, alert and worried.

~ Priori

Description tells us there is an almost storybook perfection to him and of course, we also understand that the girl loves and admires her brother.

The atmosphere or tone of a scene can also be affected by one misplaced word:

"If I fail to deliver Creana they will come for me. I cannot escape torture and murder," he thought. Stroking his bristles he looked wildly around.

~ Priori – Draft

What to do? How do I escape? Plucking at his bristles he looked around wildly.

~ Priori – Rewrite

In the original I used the word 'stroking' which sounded too much like a caress and didn't mesh with him looking 'wildly' around. It was a contradictory image and gave the wrong impression, jerking the reader out of the story. I had to show his agitation and did so by using 'plucking at his bristles'. I could have used 'tugging on them' but plucking seemed to fit his character better.

Exercise

Atmosphere is imperative to keeping your reader in the right frame of mind, like the soundtrack of a movie, which can make the heart soar as quickly as it can make it flutter in fear. It foreshadows events and taps into the unconscious of the reader, indicating the flavour of revelations to come. This exercise will help you build the appropriate atmosphere in your own work.

- Step 1: Go to your latest bit of writing and identify a place where you talk about the atmosphere rather than describe it.

- Step 2: Rewrite that section to show us exactly how creepy/deadly/mysterious that dark alley really is.

- Step 3: Now pick one of your chapters/scenes at random and look for words you have used that don't fit with how you wanted the reader to feel.

- Step 4: Take out your thesaurus and replace that incorrect word with a stronger, more emotive word. We're playing a giant game of emotional manipulation here. I give you permission to pull out all the mind control words!

The atmosphere of the Golden Moment below reflects the excitement of the characters in finding their secret tunnel as they move closer to their final destination.

Golden Moments

The glowing bodies of the worms were more pronounced in the dim sections between guttering torches. The voice of the wind chattered to us like an overexcited child, always flowing forwards as though it were our guide. The further down we went, the livelier the wind became. The flames in the torches flickered, and the light played across our features.

~ Priori

TRUST YOUR READER'S INTELLIGENCE

———

Have you ever read a book where you have the most obvious things pointed out to you by the characters? At the very least, you wonder if the characters are a little thick, because clearly they are thinking through an obvious thing a little too hard. At the worst you can't help but imagine the author standing over your shoulder going, "Did you get it? Did you get that part? Did you see what I did there? Are you sure? Really? Because I feel like you read that a little too quickly. I'm not quite sure that you understood that they didn't shiver because they were cold, but because they were *spppoookkkked by the ghooosssttttsss...*"

Contrary to popular belief your readers do understand body language, they have indeed interacted with other people in their lifetime, they can understand standard emotional reactions and know that shouts are indeed loud (returning to my *Twilight* pet peeves here). I understand the compulsion of a writer to add these little bits of 'did you get it?' into the book. You want to make sure people understand the character's emotional state. That they understand something sneaky has happened. You want them to understand the layers of meaning you've crafted. But you can do that by choosing the right word, and then trusting your reader's intelligence and your writing skills, rather than whacking them with a shovel full of repetitions. You want your readers to come back for a book that involves them, not spells everything out.

Below are several common ways a writer can insult a reader's intelligence without meaning to, in some ways it's another form of overwriting. By correcting your writing to eliminate them, you are getting your reader more involved and invested in your story.

1: Trust Your Readers Understand Body Language

There is no need to 'show' a reader your character's emotional state and then panic that they may be an idiot and decide to 'tell' them too. They're not an idiot, if they were, they wouldn't read your book. As Isobelle pointed out in my below example (the underlined words are the ones she deleted), you are making your reader passive by not forcing them to exercise their brain:

The grip on my weapon faltered and I almost dropped it <u>in shock</u>.

~ Priori – Draft

"This is the sort of thing you would cut in a second draft as it is coming to a conclusion that you want your readers to come to. Always try to trust the comprehension of an audience – as a rule of thumb, if you can figure it out, so can they. The more times you make them come to a conclusion, the more involved in your story they will be. If you tell them all the conclusions, you make them passive and so their involvement in the story will be more shallow and easier to disrupt."

~ Isobelle Carmody

2: Trust Your Readers Have the Ability to Infer Things

Readers understand that when you use certain words like 'ripped', or 'punched', or 'cut' the associated result of those actions is pain, or destruction. They can infer this because they have felt it themselves. Stating the obvious is the best way to encourage a reader to find a way to strangle you with your own book.

"I feel dirty using this magick. People died – had it ripped from them against their will."

~ Priori – Draft

"If it was ripped from them we can assume it was against their will. This sort of mistake is fine at the first and even second draft stage, but you should be constantly watching out for it, paring back, very often overwriting will be fat with unnecessary words."

~ Isobelle Carmody

*

"You have met the shadows?" His expression showed momentary surprise. His eyes flitted around the clearing but did not rest on those of the Brethren I could see beneath the trees. Somehow, I was the only one that could see them.

~ Priori – Draft

"This is unnecessary because it is obvious – let the reader infer it from the perfectly adequate information you have given them. Every time you make your reader work for information they invest something of themselves in your story."

~ Isobelle Carmody

3: Trust in YOUR Writing Skills

Many writers feel like they can never be as good as those

that have gone before them. We don't trust that what we are describing can come across as majestically as we imagined. We feel like we aren't doing it justice, and as a result we second guess ourselves, and in turn second guess the imagination of the reader, which more often than not is as imaginative as our own. So don't end a beautiful description with a throwaway line like this:

My eyes devoured <u>the sight of</u> Creana. <u>It was magnificent.</u>

~ Priori – Draft

"You have shown us this beautifully. To thus conclude it weakens the text."

~ Isobelle Carmody

The below Golden Moment is the original description she was referring to. Writing a book is an exercise in trust. Trusting that we are good enough to get across our vision and trusting that our readers are as intelligent as we think we are.

Golden Moments

How I initially missed it I don't know. The gateway we had entered was positioned directly next to the divide. Two hundred metres from the castle's gate, the cavern's earth ceiling ended abruptly. It was as though a hemisphere covered and protected the Academy and Creana; half the hemisphere was made of rock and formed the cavern roof over the Academy, the other half of the hemisphere was made of clear, thick glass and covered Creana in a giant glass dome. The join between the two materials was seamless. The glass dome extended for tens of miles. Swirling and moving outside the dome was water – the sea.

"Great goddess above," I breathed, "We are underwater."

Within the dome lay a vast white city. Thousands of houses, buildings, turrets, towers, and parks with playgrounds and waterfalls terraced down, the number of levels too plentiful to count, following the natural fall of the deepening ocean floor. The roofs were covered with dark red tiles, and the busy main thoroughfares bore little resemblance to the quiet, dusty roads of the surface.

In the middle of the city was a large, deep blue lake which overflowed at the far end. Several levels were dominated by massive pale-blue trees. The distant reaches of the town were too far away to make out details with any clarity. Alaequines, dwarfed by the landscape, flitted above the city carrying their riders to various destinations.

~ Priori

AVOIDING REPETITION

In a previous chapter I talked about repetition being the Devil. This piece of advice bears repeating (pun-high-five!). And capitalisation.

Repetition is the Devil

It does not wear Prada, but it does like flame bombing thesauruses. Writers should have it on T-shirts, badges, paintings, and written in icing on top of cupcakes. In the heat of the moment we are just trying to get words out, we pull the closest one out of our word bag and slap it on the page. It's how we manage to force ourselves through however many thousands of words in six months (or one month if you're boarding the NaNoWriMo – National Novel Writing Month – train).

But during editing you need to be vigilant as repetition

is the first thing your readers are going to pick up. It is also the easiest thing to fix. The problem is it becomes so prolific, so insidious, like a giant killer octopus working its way into your house, that repetition needs its own concentrated editing pass to remove it. I do about five editing run throughs for each of my manuscripts and one of those is dedicated to the reduction and removal of adjectives, adverbs and repetitions.

Repetition comes in more than your garden-variety mention-a-word-ten-times-in-one-page form (i.e. my use of the words 'mad glint' three times in as many paragraphs). That type is easily spotted, but the below, are less obvious:

1: Phrase Repetition

In the end I could not let the Ruhle soldiers win again. I would not let them rain destruction and terror over the world for a second time. No matter what it did to me in the end.

~ Priori – Draft

2: Partial Word Repetition

The dwindling light highlighted his high cheek bones, the soft freckles and the piercing blue eyes, alert and worried.

~ Priori – Draft

It doesn't matter that 'light', 'highlight' and 'high' are three separate words, you are essentially repeating 'light' and 'high' twice, when the sentence can easily be rewritten to avoid the clumsy word grouping. Just as you would try to avoid using 'like', 'likely' and 'likelihood' in the same sentence or paragraph.

2: Repetition of ideas/descriptions

This is a big problem for many emerging writers and is something likely to drive a reader bonkers. Say your story is set on a spaceship, and out of the 100 scenes that make up your book, 30 of those are set in the mess hall with your characters talking to each other and smiling. Repeating the same setting over and over again gives a novel the feeling of never progressing, regardless of whether or not the content of the discussion is different. You can avoid this Ground Hog Day effect in your novel by noting down the location of each of your scenes. If there are too many set in the one place (as in more than three times) look at switching up the location to somewhere new. If you're in a school, set it in a different part of the school. If they're on a ship, have them walking from one place to another and varying the tasks they do on the way.

Another writing sin that falls into this category is over-labouring a characteristic of one of your characters. E.g. stubbornness, or enthusiasm. Or you may have a tendency to highlight a particular piece of body language, or regularly repeat an action like a particular tick, or cough, or smile, or a look. My first drafts are covered in shrugs and gazes that I have to ferret out and vary least my reader curse me. Then there is the repetition of ideas.

The Golden Moment in this chapter is one of the larger types of repetition that you want to look out for, particularly if you're using some kind of system whether it be magic, technology, forensics etc. where you're explaining how something works. This moment was almost three quarters through the book and there had been many descriptions of the way the Lines of Power worked by this point. I wanted to set the scene but also avoid having a long paragraph describing things I had already described in great detail. So in that moment I made sure the description of what the Lines were doing was simple and distinct from the uses we had seen previously thus avoiding repeating myself.

So, to avoid any more repetition in this book, I shall now stop.

Golden Moments

As the water level began to descend, the delicate fabric of Lines unravelled and absorbed into the glassy floor beneath our feet.

~ Priori

CONTRADICTIONS

To infinity and beyond!

It's the catch phrase that caught the imagination of every little boy and girl under the age of twelve. Back then, all that mattered was the emotion, the hand action, the spacesuit. Dictionary meanings were things to be bent, nay moulded, to capture the idea of something with words completely contradictory to their actual meaning. These oxymorons creep into everyday life, causing slight brow furrowing for a small few, but mostly being ignored by everyone else. Frankly, the ignorers are the reason so many Norwegians leave English speaking countries confused.

I was recently asked for an 'accurate estimate' by my boss. Being a little too literal I almost laughed. Thankfully the little 'ignore' warning belatedly flared in my brain and I kept my job. If I didn't ignore all the 'seriously-funny's, 'bitter-sweet's, 'irregular-pattern's, 'original-copy's, 'small-crowd's, 'liquid-gas's and 'deafening-silence's I would be lacking half a dozen friends by now. And potentially have gained two or three more dogs. I wonder if it's not my annoyance with contradictory phrases that has me avoiding zombie flicks; the phrase 'living-dead' defies logic.

Contradictions crop up a lot in drafts, though most are subtler than 'deafening-silence' and are easily missed by a writer immersed in their world. Deafening-silence is a contradiction of word meaning, but contradictions come in many more forms. Writers need to be vigilant because they are one of the biggest causes of throwing a reader out of the story. You don't want them using their 'say what?' face. What you want is the reader tripping over their own eyeballs to find out what happens at the end.

In one paragraph I had read and revised at least two dozen times in *Priori*, I never once picked out the contradiction below until Isobelle highlighted it:

As the distance grew between us and the soldiers, so did the weight of my fear. Somehow something was amiss. We had seen the soldiers pass yet... I suddenly remembered a disturbing fact Charlie had once told me. The Ruhle usually travelled in groups of seven...

~ Priori – Draft

"Wouldn't Charlie know, especially if he is as alert as he seems? He's standing right next to her. Can someone else have told her?"

~ Isobelle Carmody

In the scene, the main character's brother, Charlie, has given the go ahead to sneak out of their hiding place, but Beverly senses something is off. Yet if he's the one who's told her how many soldiers there should be, why would he not act on that knowledge?

Natural reader conclusion? He's a few peanuts short of an elephant snack or the writer's not paying attention. Let's just say making my protagonist's brother look like an ass was not in the character profile. Now, in the final draft, an old teacher of Beverly's is attributed to this plot device. This subtle inconsistency, a small contradiction in the scheme of things, almost derailed the characterisation of one of my main characters in the third page.

Identifying contradictions is essential to the believability of your world. Otherwise readers will dismiss your characters as cardboard cut-outs. So comb your writing with your new-found awareness, young Obi-One. But be warned, your superhero perception of oxymorons may make you unpopular at parties. Until then, perhaps it's best to confine your superpowers to writing and act natural...

What started this little obsession? Check out the *Extremely Loud, Incredibly Close* clip below:

https://youtu.be/WQQ1oGmCoeE

Exercise

Spotting contradictions isn't too difficult, but re-writing them to say what you mean can be. Hopefully the below exercise will help with that.

- Step 1: Pick 3-4 contradictions from the video link above and rewrite them so you get the meaning across without contradicting yourself. Only write 2-3 sentences max for each one.

SAY SOMETHING TRUE - CLICHÉS IN DIALOGUE

Genre writers love a bit of drama; we are the kings and queens of drama. We are so used to having American or British accents declare do-or-die statements that it's become part of our psyche. Those are the little voices that ring in our head when we write dialogue, they sound impressive, we write them down. Yet these vague and clichéd pronouncements when you really look at them have no substance, at the very least they amount to unhelpful advice, at the most they're just fun to shout at your enemies. But if our characters and their enemies *really* lived, these phrases are more likely to induce laughter rather than fear.

As writers, when we are not quite sure of the truth of the moment we fall back on clichés, when we should be avoiding them like a teen love song, locking them in a box, throwing away the key, collapsing a cave on the box and for good measure, probably setting it on fire. You know the sort of pronouncements I'm talking about, I certainly found some in my manuscript:

All that was good and beautiful seemed to die in that moment when death won.

~ Priori – Draft

Seriously? That's a little melodramatic isn't it? And more than a little untrue. Death doesn't win, it's a natural force (unless it's not, then you've got some serious world building to do). Clichés are those vague pronouncements that litter genre novels, and replace what should be said at important moments with generalisations that add no meaning to the story. The biggest cliché Isobelle found in my work was a sentence I repeated several times throughout my manuscript because I thought it was *the* sentence that defined Beverly and was her mantra for strength.

Destiny comes when one does not expect it. All you can do is accept it with grace, courage, wisdom and faith.

~ Priori – Draft

Oh it was profound, it was impressive, it was a pile of meaningless crap. As I had correctly identified, it was a super important moment, but if you truly looked at the sentence it had very little meaning. It was the sort of cliché that is rife in fantasy (and gives fantasy a bad name). 'Destiny comes', what is destiny but the future, and it is always coming, each choice and small moment leading onto the next. And was Beverly's teacher really telling Beverly this list of high virtues because he thought an eighteen year old could respond to something that scares the hell out of her, with 'grace, courage, wisdom and faith'? Of course not! I don't think any teenager in their right mind would claim this as good, reassuring advice, even a fictional one. They'd tell you to go jump first and report back to them on how it went. It took me a while to come to grips with the fact that a good story doesn't need a catch phrase, it needs the right truth in that moment.

As Isobelle said:

"I think you need to find a deeper more honest way to express the gravity of the moment than these words. Find something stronger for her to be told here, a thing that might be said to a soldier about to go out to face a war that will likely kill him, and yet which he must fight. Not platitudes or a cliché, but something true."

~ Isobelle Carmody

That something true changed in each moment that silly proclamation appeared.

The main component where clichés will always find a way into your work is dialogue. Dialogue is a part of characterisation and clichés add nothing to the character. With any piece of dialogue you should be asking yourself, what are you trying to express about your characters here? Is anything real expressed or are they speaking only so you can convey information to your audience? If so then a precise explanation is more efficient than dialogue. If you have dialogue, it must add to our understanding of the character. Unless the point is that you character offers trite homilies and clichés instead of heartfelt comments or grim silence or genuine reassurances. Yes, clichés at times can be fine but *only* if they tell us something about the character. Very rarely do writers do this well, so it's best avoided in general. Here are a couple of my 'clichés' so you can get a feel for them:

Sometimes we are faced with hard decisions in life, we approach them as best we can but we cannot always get it right. Just remember why we are doing this. It won't get easier, but hopefully in time you will be able to move on.

~ Cliché: Priori – Draft

"Don't you see? It was the betrayer that caused those deaths.

We cannot always get it right, as much as we might plan and hope til we are sick. I wish I could take that horrible feeling away for you."

~ Priori – Rewrite

The original dialogue was a series of trite clichés, when one real sounding sentence of reassurance would be far more effective.

When the soldiers pass out of earshot we must ride as swiftly as the wind.

~ Cliché: Priori – Draft

Don't turn your back on the world because the road of life becomes more challenging. Only you can make your life count. Promise me you'll try, don't give up now.

~ Cliché: Priori – Draft

The sentences before and after a moment of pain, fear and distress in the text sound trite.

"The outcome is always clouded," I said, my voice sharp. "My knowledge is too limited, I don't know how to seek such a destiny."

~ Cliché: Priori – Draft

At times it was necessary and proper for her to speak more formally, but here it was better that she spoke as Beverly and a young woman. 'Seek such a destiny' is a cliché and meaningless. Far better to have her say, 'I can't do what you want! I don't know how!'

Do you have trite or overused expressions in your writing? Or a character whose dialogue is predictable? These are clichés. They are not restricted to sayings such as 'strong as an ox' or 'sadder but wiser', they are words and phrases that have become overused to the point of losing their original meaning.

Be on the lookout for those golden bits of dialogue in your writing, words that are wise, true and feel real, and try to emulate them elsewhere.

Exercise

Clichés are those awkward phrases that you hear in almost every Hollywood movie, the words or phrases that have become so overused to the point of losing meaning.

- Step 1: Practise rewriting a cliché by taking one of the ones in this chapter and making it less

---

flippant, and more original.

- Step 2: Then, go cliché hunting in your first scene. Look for clichés like 'strong as an ox' or stereotypical dialogue from characters.

- Step 3: Rewrite these clichés so that they are less trite and more realistic.

In the Golden Moment below the Headmaster of the Academy Beverly attends could have descended into all types of clichés about being brave. A good balance was struck here in sticking with themes of courage while at the same time avoiding the regular clichés (hopefully you agree with Isobelle's assessment on this!).

Golden Moments

"Beverly," the commanding tone in Elitree's voice forced me to look up. He regarded me with a stern sympathy. "I know what is going through your mind but you have to hold those feelings at bay. Courage isn't the absence of fear but the will to go on in the face of fear. We knew what we were doing when we took you in."

~ Priori

WRITING DIALECT SUBTLY

Oh, top o' tha mornin' to ye wee lasses an' laddies. I be' ye dinna 'spect ta see this wee chapter in thick Scots, dinna ye? Noo, how lang wull ye carry on wi' it I wunder?

Certainly not past the fourth sentence, so I'll save you the pain of imagining me with the Scottish accent from hell. It's funny, as I read that phonetic dialect above I can hear the accent of a local university lecturer, Lee, prattling on in my head. He has one of the thickest accents you have ever heard, all *wee's* and *Ai's* and half formed words that sound like they are being performed around a golf ball. It's immensely fun to listen to. But at the same time, as I read the dialect above, I realise it's taken me double time (literally, 15 seconds with accent, to 8 seconds without) to get to the end of this cultural explosion. Suddenly, I am distinctly aware of the fact I am reading (at the pace of a snail, on the back of a tortoise, on the back of a Galapagos Island turtle) rather than concentrating on a good story.

There seems to be this belief with genre writers (fantasy in particular) that accents *must* appear as they sound, that it makes them seem real, that it makes the character come to life, that it helps build the world. Yes, I too was a part of this club that subconsciously aims to make a reader's head explode. But all excessive, spelt-out dialect does, is make the reader aware that they are reading, rather than being allowed to live the story.

I understand why authors do it; Kate Forsyth in her Witches of Eileanan series used dialect a lot. She thought it was really important to show the Scottish heritage present in her fantasy world, and dialect was the way she decided to do this. However, the majority of readers hated it – with one reader noting that everyone in the book was talking with the same accent, so what was the point of making a big deal about the pronunciation? It didn't add anything to the characterisation, it slowed down the reader's reading pace. '*I wish now that I hadn't done it, or at least done it a lot more softly,*' Kate has said in more than one interview.

Usually a peculiar way of speaking is a short cut to showing that a character is from a foreign place, or is separated from everyone else by a class system. But less emphasis should be placed on phonetic spelling of the accented words, and more on the syntax (word choice and phrasing) that would match the character's manner of speech, and describing how the accent sounds, like I did with Lee's accent above and the sentences below:

"She noticed he spoke with a slight accent. Not quite American, not quite Irish. It was the sort of thing you only heard when he was stressed or angry, but it was there."

Luckily, in *Priori*, I only had one minor character and a couple of 'extras' with dialogue that had the power to stop a reader in their tracks like a crash-test dummy. Isobelle picked them up straight away.

"There's b'en a sight'n! Hurry! Don' forget, capture 'er alive."

~ Priori – Draft

"If you want to suggest a dialect, try to do it with less changes as it makes the text hard to read and hard to understand."

~ Isobelle Carmody

"There's been a sighting! Hurry! Don' forget, take 'im alive," a growling voice said.

~ Priori – Rewrite

*

"My name is Olimpan an' the headmasta' was ask'n me to wake ye up for breakfast righ'."

~ Priori – Draft

"This dialogue jars for me ... Why are there different dialects by the way? Did you explain that, and I missed it?"

~ Isobelle Carmody

"Excuse me, dinna mean to scare you. My name is Olimpan and the Master was asking me to wake you for breakfast, righ'."

~ Priori – Rewrite

While it may seem authentic to you, a reader will not thank you for making them use their brain to try and understand what the character is saying when ultimately, it adds nothing major to the story. So do yourself a favour, 'lighten' it up!

Exercise

Have you ever read a piece of dialect that had you feel like you were trying to speak with nails in your throat? The

---

below exercise will help you get a grip on dialects in your own work.

Part 1

Clean up the below phonetically spelt dialogue and jot down two to three different ways you could describe the accent in the text around the dialogue.

- A redneck: "How a-bow-ou ah-nudder 'un?"

- A cowboy: "Yeah, you betcha der, chieftain. Goin' down wit dat der new fella, don'tcha know, and we'll git dat der whole kit and kaboodle up the shaft der lickety split. "

- From Huckleberry Finn: "Oh, Huck, I bust out a-cryin' en grab her up in my arms, en say, 'Oh, de po' little thing! De Lord God Amighty fogive po' ole Jim, Kaze he never gwyne to fogive hisself as long's he live!' Oh, she was plumb deef en dumb, Huck, plumb deef en dumb – en I'd ben atreat'n her so!

- A Scotsman: "Ah dinnae ahsk fer mae dinnah tae be tan minuts lat, nae did I, Mae wicket lahssie?"

- A French woman: "No dinnar for you, monsieur! I do not zink you are funeee. You scoundrelles are all ze zame! Zis is a scandael!"

Part 2

Ferret it out in your own writing, be ruthless! Replace any phonetic dialect with short descriptors of the sound of the accent rather than trying to reproduce it. While accent adds character you don't need to allude to it in every chapter. That becomes repetitive.

The Golden Moment below does involve a male character with a very polite and posh accent, but I thought it better to focus on the comedy of the moment and the character's quirky personality rather than the way he delivered it.

Golden Moments

"So you want me to say level three. That's all, just say it?" I asked.
"Loudly if you don't mind," he said mildly, *"Sometimes, it hears wrong."*

~ Priori

SHOW DON'T TELL – IT'S FUNNIER THAT WAY

If you've attended a writing course you will no doubt be familiar with the whole show-don't-tell diatribe. But what you may not know, is that the show-don't-tell thing isn't as obvious as you first think. For those of you who are not familiar with this notion, consider the difference between telling your friends a story about something funny that happened and then showing them a video of it. The first (telling) does all the work for your mate, makes them lazy, and relies on them trusting your judgement enough to believe that it was, in fact, the most hilariously funny thing that's ever happened in the history of the world. Ever. The second (showing) allows your mate to become *involved*. The second blasts the first into outer space and then throws rotten tomatoes at it.

To give you an example, there was this *hilarious* video

I watched the other day, god I almost swallowed my own tongue I was laughing so hard. It was this video of a squirrel, but someone had done this voice over, and the squirrel was yelling, "Alan! Alan! Alan!" and then he's all like, "No wait, that's not Alan, that's Steve! Steve! Steve! Steve!" And then he gets all confused again and is like, "Alan! Alan! Alan!" It was so flipping funny I almost died.

Rather than forcing you to read that paragraph, I should have sent you straight to this YouTube link (https://youtu.be/XgvR3y5JCXg). Show, don't tell, case in point!

When I first started my mentorship with Isobelle I had done all of the prerequisite beginner writing courses (probably like you), and I thought I had show-don't-tell in the bag! I could slam dunk that baby while blindfolded, fighting off three ninjas and battling a shark with a fricken laser beam on its head. But I hadn't noticed that show-don't-tell wasn't just about the big scenes and the fancy cars, it was also about the minute word choices we make.

"I am here," repeated the unnatural voice, not quite there, not quite sane.

~ Priori – Draft

"Using the word 'unnatural' is labelling. Unnatural how? And then you use 'not quite sane'. How can she tell this? Or is it simply

that irrational certainty that sometimes comes in dreams? If so, say so."

~ Isobelle Carmody

*

His cruel face...

~ Priori – Draft

"Why cruel? This is one of those things in fantasy we have to guard ourselves from – labelling. Instead of saying he is cruel, simply describe his face and let the audience come up with the word."

~ Isobelle Carmody

At the landing where the two staircases divided stood a tall, stiff man with smooth-cropped black hair neatly parted to one side. His narrow face housed an icy expression and darting green eyes with the half mad glint of one on the verge of losing his sanity. But the madness could not hide the identity of the haggard man.

~ Priori – Rewrite

We naturally label as part of life, and it makes sense that this would find its way, like an insidious weed, into our writing. In a way, show-don't-tell comes in two flavours, labelling, and the more well known, being a lazy writer who can't be bothered filling in the back story.

Hatred shone in her eyes as the words tumbled from her mouth without pause. She poured out sorrow built up after so many years.

~ Priori – Draft

"Cut this. Let the words show themselves as tumbling out, let us hear the sorrow pour out rather than having it announced to us."

~ Isobelle Carmody

Her back stiffened, her eyes boring into mine. It was as though I had unlocked a forbidden door. Hatred shone in her eyes as the words tumbled from her mouth. "The man was ignorant and foolish just like you!" she spat.

My heart constricted. "No! He was wise and good!" I cried, "He loved us!" Trembling, I could feel the small red spider vein burning on my cheek.

"How would you know? He didn't even try to see you when you were born! All you need to know is he did not care enough! He never loved you! He never loved me! If he had, he wouldn't have allowed himself to be killed. Just get out! Get away from me!" She shrieked.

~ Priori – Rewrite

The original line was from the second chapter in the book. At that point the reader doesn't yet trust the main character, Beverly. And so the character telling us that her mother spilled out past sorrow has very little impact. It is hollow. The rewrite above is a much more powerful way of showing her mother's sorrow. It also adds drama to the scene. It gives us a reason to hate Beverly's mother as much as she does.

So the next time you tell a reader about the moment your brother got his nuts squashed because he leapt over a pole without enough Gummy Berry Juice, give them the full length movie rather than the trailer.

Exercise

Replace the telling by describing/showing at least three of the below labels:

- <u>Cruel</u> face,
- <u>Untrustworthy</u> man,
- <u>Untrustworthy</u> woman,
- She had a <u>canny</u> face,
- <u>Evil</u> smile,
- <u>Unnatural</u> noise,

- She was a <u>geek</u>,

- He was a <u>weirdo</u>,

- The glen had a <u>magical</u> feel,

- The creature was <u>unreal</u>,

- The whole scenario was so <u>surreal</u>.

In the below Golden Moment I could have *told* the readers the fabric between worlds was full of distortions, but they wouldn't have *seen* it. Showing what was causing the distortions and what they acted like gave a much stronger visual.

Golden Moments

I marvelled that I could actually feel all the distortions in the threads of the fabric; people entering and leaving and at regular intervals I could feel the earth tremors vibrate through, like a wave drowning out all the other magickal pulses.

~ Priori

IF YOU'RE NOT A POET, YOU SHOULD KNOW IT, & MOVE ON!

Chances are as a reader of genre you may have come across an elvish song or poem, or a saying/prophecy of epic-doom in the novels you've read. It's a trope and Tolkien is probably to blame. Don't get me wrong, his stories are amazing, but I could have done with less of the 'look-at-how-much-imagination-I-have-I-shall-explode-your-minds' parts (of course the books are of their time, and writing has evolved since then). If you are unfamiliar with the purpose of a song or prophecy, (which are normally poetic) here is a short list of uses:

- **A Song is never JUST a song** Normally it contains *great knowledge for your quest* and performs the same function as a *legend*. Your character as such should attend to the words, the tune is not important (obviously, it's a book mate, not a musical).

- A Song can also be *a historical lesson of great importance*. It may tell you why you shouldn't eat that berry, or lick that toad, or trust a house made of candy. They are rarely put in there for shits and giggles (unless you are writing a parody fantasy, then apply the trope liberally and with much tongue in cheek action).

- A Prophecy is used by Management to make sure no character or reader is surprised by events. Well... it depends on how good you are at riddles, but that's the general gist. All prophecies come true, them's da rules. Even if you only get the meaning of the prophecy after everything goes to hell in a hand basket. You can fit any meaning you like to words that don't make sense and include a few key nouns. Methods of delivery include: sages, mystics, crystal balls, dreams, mirrors, pools, lakes, ruins, cards, omens, astrology, time travellers, and crazy beggars.

You may have gathered from the list above that these

additions to a fantasy world are a little cliché, but kind of expected. It's something to be aware of so you never have to have your writing group give you this advice:

> "Of course the poem needs work, Emily. Unless you are a poet, I would tend to make it poetic prose – it will be easier to make it sound good and you will be freed from having to force the meter. Or one of them has to comment that it is not a very good poem – if you want to make it a poem, you must work it up into a real poem."

~ Isobelle Carmody

What was Isobelle referring to? This little gem:

First think of where the sea and the sky are one
And unlike any other, the clouds across the sea are none
The opening of the whale's mouth is where it lays
The entrance to the city, deepest of deep blue, in all its days
The mouth swallows you up, right down to the tail
Where a thumb is sticking up has a bright copper nail
The nail moves when pulled with the wind
Be quick, be smart, and get down there soon
Before the Scorpion finds you.

~ Priori – Draft

Yeah, you can kind of tell I gave up in that last couple of lines. But still, it didn't matter right?? It was the *knowledge* that counted didn't it? It was only a small, cheesy part of a greater whole, surely. But after several months of mentorship with Isobelle, I knew I was kidding myself. No bit of your manuscript should escape your quest for perfection (see, even authors have quests).

After I finished crying in a curled up ball for half an hour I finally accepted I'm not a poet, and probably never will be. A mix of rhythmic genius and lyrical words does not live inside my heart, my head or my fingers. It doesn't get under my skin and make me write prose that has people ripping off their clothes and giving them to the homeless. The above was supposed to be a road map, a set of clues to where the characters needed to be. Instead the reader gets some very bad poetry whose meaning is thick as mud. So following Isobelle's advice and turning it into 'poetic' prose, we end up with this, more palatable version of the map/knowledge-of-great-fate:

"The city is a jewel surround by midnight blue, and nigh impenetrable by land and sea. It is the largest and deepest of its ilk, bordered by deadly currents and tangled forest. It is the only place the dauntless Airships cannot fly. To find the entrance you must first search for where the sea and the sky are one and the clouds across the sea are none. There, the mouth of the Whale will swallow you to its tail. Then seek the thumb with the bright copper

nail which moves with the wind. Make haste through the passage,
swift as the breeze, before the Scorpion finds you."

~ Priori – Rewrite

There was another poem lurking in the back end of my manuscript, it got pretty much the same feedback, I won't burn your eyes with that one. I did attempt for a time to learn the art of poetry, what it was that made a poem stop stinking like dead fish. But the problem was, I don't understand most poetry, I'm never quite sure what is going on, and as I noted before, you should really avoid having stanzas in your words for funsies. Poets, I am not your target audience.

It was time to concede defeat and realise that unless I was inhabited by the ghost of Banjo Patterson or Dorothea MacKellar, it was best to stick to what I was good at and leave poetry to the people who won't massacre it then bury it in the forest. If you're not a poet don't torture your readers. Based on my previous attempts can you imagine how terrible my poem version of the Golden Moment for this chapter would have been? Yes, you're right, best not dwell on that thought. As a writer, you need to stick to the forms that you're good at, with everything else you've got to attend a couple of therapy sessions and move on.

Golden Moments

Icy wind assaulted us accompanied by a driving rain, which hid all features behind its cold curtain. The air was charged with an electricity brought on by only the worst of storms. The bay lit up in a brief moment of radiance as green lightning cracked the sky.

~ Priori

YOU CAN DISAGREE... WITH A VALID REASON

If you ask any professional writer what the hardest thing is about the writing process, what is most discouraging, what kicks you in the stomach harder than a donkey flipping out on bad mushrooms, they will tell you it's the day you get your edits back from your editor. Or the day you get feedback from you mentor, or beta reader, or writers' group, or grammar-Nazi of a grandmother. Seeing all those marks, all that red and crossing out is enough to make even the toughest pen monkey do one of two things: a) curl up into a ball in a corner, or; b) plan the number of ways they can get back at the bastards. Sometimes it's so hard you want to give it all up and go back to your previous and more attainable dream of being an astronaut and riding space monkeys through the cosmos.

When you get feedback you always have to weigh up

how *right* it actually is, how much experience the beta reader has and whether or not you trust that experience. For example, though she means well and has a strong grasp of language from the era where you'd get rapped on the knuckles by a cane if you got it wrong, my grammar-Nazi of a grandmother would probably have less understanding of what I was writing (*How exactly are these horses flying? You do realise this is physically impossible. One rap for overactive imagination*) than my mentor Isobelle who is one of Australia's most awarded fantasy authors.

It's tough to know when you should stand your ground and when your ego is getting in the way of a good story. I use the below classification to help me make the decision on what to change:

- Is the piece of feedback from a person whose lifelong passion and profession is editing? If yes, then they probably know what they're talking about, rate their words highly.

- Is this piece of feedback from someone who claims they are awesome at editing (they even have the degree!) but haven't actually ever had a job as a proper editor? Then I'd take their words with a grain of salt, technical knowledge doesn't always translate, particularly if you're writing genre rather than high-brow literary fiction.

- Is the feedback from an author who has won at least three awards for their work? High on the, they-probably-know-what-they're-talking-about, scale.

- When you look at that piece of feedback, do you instantly recognise that's exactly what your manuscript needs but previously you couldn't: a) articulate what had to change; b) admit it needed changing because you'd already rewritten that section ten times and frankly you were about ready to make your manuscript into a paper hat instead. Well now you've had some distance from the piece and some outside perspective, so hop to that editing.

- Is the feedback from a reader of that genre? Then while I wouldn't take their nitty-gritty line edits as gospel, I would be paying attention to any part where they didn't understand exactly what was happening, or they didn't connect with a main character.

- Is the feedback from a reader who doesn't normally read that genre (hello Mum!)? Ok, so you can probably ignore the 'I don't understand how that airship flies or how piranhas are carnivorous aliens' comments, lest you start over explaining things. Focus more on the comments where they say they can't *see* the scene, or get a clear image of a character. These comments are going to let you know if your character *motivations* and sense of *place* are coming though clearly.

There will always be instances where you don't agree with a comment, because frankly, you understand physics better than them (in my case). Or sewing, or candle stick making, or the decomposition of human bodies, or penetration depth of cactus needles into the human buttock. There is no rule written, unwritten, or carved into stone that says you can't argue with edits from a person of high esteem, if you have a valid reason and have done your research thoroughly. Not because you like the word, or the sentence, or that smart-arse one line, but because it is exactly the *right* word or action or character motivation or fact.

It was very rare that I disagreed with the edits and suggestions offered by Isobelle (well...once I'd calmed down and stopped plotting the number of ways I could do damage with a pen), but the below are two cases where I was adamant that these were the right words and descriptions for that moment:

A thread of light streaked from the line in his fingers as though following some invisible trajectory. It arced swiftly like a wave

*through water from one cave to the next before connecting with
the hilt of Charlie's weapon.*

~ Priori – Draft

"*A wave would not arc. This description does not work because
you cannot imagine a line of light moving in an arc, which is not
like a wave unless it widens and flattens, in which case say that.
Try to find a better way to describe its movement. When in doubt,
simplify and use strong, clear, basic words, add the frills later if
you feel you need them.*"

~ Isobelle Carmody

*Lifting his arm to chest height, the boy pinched the space in
front of him and a short glowing line appeared from thin air. His
other hand clenched a neck charm hanging around his throat.
Muttering, he flicked his finger, jerking the glowing string taut. A
thread of light streaked from the line, as though following some
invisible trajectory. It arced like a speeding wave before
connecting with Charlie's weapon. The sword went flying across
the room.*

~ Priori – Rewrite

You'll note that while I did simplify the sentence, I did
not in fact remove the word 'arc'. That is because I know
from my maths and physics lectures that waves come in
more forms than waves through water, they come as sine

214

and cosine waves or the compression waveforms of sound, all of which are made up of arcs of various radiuses linked together. Even a wave through water when shown in cross section moves in massive concave and convex arcs. This glowing line of magic is essentially travelling like a sine wave through the air, and as sine waves are not called that (or even known or studied) in this fantasy world, the word 'arc' does quite nicely to describe this particular movement.

The violent tremor pitched me forward, the shaking earth squealing and groaning in protest.

~ Priori – Draft

"Squealing is too strange a word to use – unless there is an explanation why it would sound like that."

~ Isobelle Carmody

Having worked in mining for almost three years and having studied geology for four, I can tell you with the utmost confidence that rocks do in fact squeal as they scrape with extreme force against each other. It is akin to the sound of nails on a blackboard and happens much more frequently than 'groaning' in a high stress environment. It is not the sound you want to hear whether you're underground or above ground because it means you are in deep doo-doo.

While you should never let ego get in the way of a good story, there are some things you are going to feel strongly about. And then there will the moments like this chapter's Golden Moment where you can make things so fantastical, no one can really argue with you about its components. The point is to weigh your experience against the experience of the person giving you feedback, and if yours has the hospital bills and cactus pockmarks to prove it, don't be afraid to stand your ground.

Golden Moments

I prised the cut open with my fingers, revealing a sliver of the black void with its sparkling rain.

~ Priori

Where to Now?

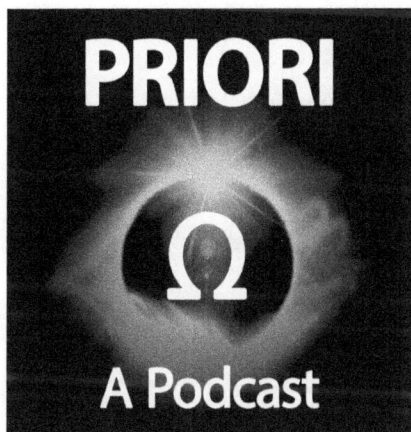

While this is the end of the lessons I learnt from Isobelle this is not the end of my exploration of writing, nor my experimentation with *Priori*. (Sorry to all those who thought they could get rid of me, I'm like a fungus, I just keep growing.) I'll still be passing on writing tools that I have learnt, and ways to expand your writing further on my website Craven Stories http://www.cravenstories.com. But more excitingly, I have completed a podcast version of the *Priori* manuscript, 28 episodes of awesome voice acting and fun.

I banded together with the amazing voiceover talents of Kevin Powe, Colin Smith, Sam Piaggio, and Lois Spangler, and the editing talents of David Phythian, to turn *Priori* into this audio extravaganza for your listening pleasure. The full episodes are out now and available on iTunes or cravenstories.com, but you can keep an eye out for further developments of *Priori* and its (hopefully) future publication in print, by signing up to the Reader Freebies newsletter at Craven Stories.

Signing up to the newsletter also gets you access to review copies of my novels, short stories, and other giveaways and competitions across the year.

Good luck on your writing journey. I can't wait to read *your* original fantasy.

If You Enjoyed, Please, Leave a Review Online!

The only way authors can make a living from their work is if more people know about it, and the best way to help out an author you enjoyed is to leave a review! I really appreciate your support. And please, don't hesitate to email me either.

Review @ Goodreads: http://bit.ly/OriginalFantasy

Thank you! And good luck in your own writing journey.

Other Books By Emily

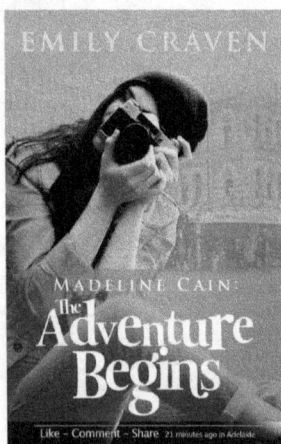

The first book in The Grand Adventures of Madeline Cain series. A contemporary comedy written as though you're reading the main character's Facebook page. While this isn't fantasy, it's still a fun read from Emily Craven.

***

Life after high-school is looming and Madeline Cain is freaking out. Everyone has an opinion on what she should do with her life but her. What sane person decides the rest of their life at 17?

As Maddie resigns herself to six months of decision-making hell she meets Claire; an exchange student from Ireland with a wicked sense of humour and an aversion to technology. Claire convinces Maddie to join her '365 Days of Fun' project and suddenly Maddie finds herself giving fake tarot readings at the beach, dressing up as a superhero to stop petty crime, and hijacking a cult from its creator.

But when Madeline gets caught 'playing games' rather than taking her future 'seriously', reality comes crashing down. Will Maddie find the career of her dreams? Or is she doomed to spend her life adventure-less?

Download it now, for free, from your favourite ebook store. Or you can purchase a print copy from your favourite online store. While I wish I could say the print book was free, paper, ink and shipping still cost money, soooo... if you do decide to go the paper back route, thanks for your support!

Ebook Revolution The Ultimate Guide To Ebook Success

Available at all online book stores in print and ebook.

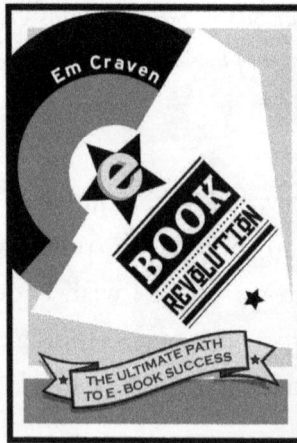

While every author's ultimate dream is to sniff the glue binding of the crisp, off-white pages of their first glossy masterpiece, the reality is that most of us will never write a book that exactly fits a publisher's idea of a mainstream, marketable novel. However, with almost nine million searches per month for 'e-books' on Google and 2.5 million searches for 'free e-books', we would be out of our minds not to capitalise on this digitisation of our industry.

E-book Revolution: The Ultimate Guide To E-book Success demonstrates **how to take those critical first steps to e-book success** and choose the right e-book model and promotion style for you. It covers everything you need to know about the e-book revolution, readying and formatting your manuscript for sale, and marketing your work to the world. Learn innovative ways to make your e-book unique, **how to boost author sales,** connect with your readers so they beg for more and promote your work without paying a cent in advertising. **Discover the hidden truth behind why publishers reject perfectly good manuscripts.**

Emily Craven has been researching author marketing and the e-book revolution for almost a decade and has presented on the subject for organisations across the world. Join Emily Craven for the education YOU need!

About Emily

Chocolate. Karaoke. Star Trek. Travel. Books. Puppies. Shaking what your Mama gave you. All of these are some of my favourite things. But when I meet someone, I want to know who they are, not what they like. I want to know what's their story? Why do they get up every morning? Other than, like, needing to have a pee.

Aherm, moving on.

For me, what rocks my world is showing daring creatives

how to draw the curious down the rabbit hole with stories, how to use their tales to spark connection, understanding, and create belonging with a wonderland of their making.

Stories entered my DNA as a kid. They were what saved me from lonely lunch times with no friends when my family moved states and I was shoved into a new school mid-year, mid-puberty, mid-awkward-phase. They allowed me to escape to another world of adventure, of struggle (that wasn't mine), of empathy, perspective, and heroes who strived against the bullies, and again and again, picked themselves. Stories showed me how to adapt, to care, to trust myself. They understood me on a level I barely understood myself. I was such a voracious reader I started writing my own books when I was 12 because my favourite authors just couldn't keep up.

Stories were how I survived boredom. Boredom was how I ended up a Star Trek nerd. Every afternoon when I got home from school, my mother commandeered the TV to fuel her Star Trek addiction. The choice was be bored or be obsessed. You could say I was brain-washed a Trekkie and I have no regrets!

That's the only reason I can think of for how I ended up choosing to study Astrophysics. Two years in and something happened that I never in a million years expected. I hated it. I had no idea what else I would even do if I quit. I was good at it, sure, but every six months I would have a mini-break-down in my bedroom, the words of high-school teachers and parents going around and round my head – 'you're too smart for art.' If present me could time travel, I'd go back and slap them all up-side the head, with a loud, 'fuck that noise' for good measure.

How many times have you been told you 'should'? You should do this, you should do that, even though you know that box doesn't fit you?

What I didn't realise at the time was the reason I was so drawn to Star Trek wasn't the science, it was the adventure. A soap opera in space; people working together solving problems, falling in love, and shooting phasers! This was the root of my unhappiness; I was suppressing the biggest part of myself. I didn't want knowledge for the sake of knowledge, I want to create things that connected people. And the way that excited me, that lit a fire in my belly to create that connection, was by creating and sharing stories. Fictional preferably, with a hint of magic, a dash of quirky, and a sneaky side of truth.

I wish I could tell you that when I set my sights on career as storyteller, I shook off that 'should' energy. I did not. While I devoured dozens of courses on writing, publishing, marketing, editing and eBooks, and learnt one of the most important lessons of my life – that what you create alone will never be as good as what you'll create together with the feedback of professionals who aren't you and see your blind spots – I was still doing all the things you should. You should send your novels to traditional publishers, you should write short stories to get a name for yourself, you should have a 'very' professional website where you're 'very serious' and therefore 'competent', as confirmed by your head shot which makes you look like you have sat on a cactus.

I waited a really long time for someone to pick me. And I was lonely, so very very lonely. When a boy who already had a 3-book deal with a major publisher got the only writing grant available in the state to writers under 30, something finally snapped for me. I was sick of waiting; it was time to choose myself. I couldn't be rejected if I was the one creating the thing, right?

It was when I took the conscious decision to step off the beaten path that things changed for me. I created my own opportunities, but in a way that no one else was doing at the time – I created them so that I was making and creating WITH someone else. The power of collaboration runs through everything I do now, from the very first writing and publishing project I created in my little city of Adelaide, which spiralled into a 5-year international endeavour that would turn into the award-winning storytelling app, Story City, and lift up over 300 storytellers across half a dozen creative industries.

In creating my own opportunities, in making things like Story City, my novels, my branding work, I realised I made a place where I belonged, and where hundreds and thousands of others realised they belonged.

The success that I have had today is due largely to the power of story. Of how stories allow you to be understood for you, and to connect beyond yourself. I've won awards, presented hundreds of hours of storytelling workshops internationally, published 6 books, edited and/or published dozens of authors, I am a global entrepreneur of an app that helps you explore and connect to a city and the stories of its people, and I'm part of a 6 person team that brands a handful of high-flying femmpreneurs every year.

While much of that has been because of hard work, talent, and practice, the truth of the matter is I have gotten this far because I have chosen to make things together, rather than alone. To hone my understanding, skills and stories, with outside eyes, because through collaboration I make far more impact than I ever would on my own.

So I say to you pick yourself, don't wait for others to pick you. But also pick doing it together, rather than doing it alone.

Find your people. Band together. And you will make great things.

Contact

Facebook: *http://www.facebook.com/EmilyCravenAuthor*
Website (bookmark me!): *http://www.cravenstories.com*
Twitter: *@cravenstories*
Instagram: *@imagesforjoy*
Work With Me: http://www.cravenstories.com/work-with-me/